"My faith is strengthened and my [...] after reading *A Thousand Times Yes.* [...] the life experiences of these two courageous doctors—my parents— Dr. Wana Ann and Dr. Giles Fort (and my friends may find out a few things I didn't even know!)
—DR. GORDON FORT, senior vice-president, Prayer Mobilization and Training, International Mission Board of the Southern Baptist Convention

"Long before our arrival in Zimbabwe, we had heard of Drs. Giles and Wana Ann Fort. Their names were always spoken with an unusual degree of respect bordering on reverence, and their work in Rhodesia (now Zimbabwe) was of the nature most associated with missionary pioneers of a bygone era. In *A Thousand Times Yes*, you can read Dr. Fort's gripping account of missionary service. We are among those privileged to have been touched by their lives. Now, in these pages, you can experience that life-changing touch as well."
—TOM AND JEANNIE ELLIFF, president, International Mission Board of the Southern Baptist Convention, and former missionary colleagues of the Forts

"*A Thousand Times Yes* is a beautiful tribute to a life lived out of obedience to Christ. As you read, you will feel like you have met this faithful servant of God who passes on just some of her millions of stories with grace and Southern charm. Dr. Wana Ann is strikingly down-to-earth and real, helping you realize that if you will be faithful to God and will act in obedience, He will be faithful and do great things through you. I am proud to add Dr. Wana Ann to my list of heroes."
—CHARLES FIELDING, MD, author of *Preach and Heal*

"Wow! I just finished reading this wonderful book. I have been transported in time, transfixed as I read Wana Ann's incredible story. I don't know when I have ever read nonstop like I did today. I was moved to tears many times as I remembered the hard times. I could even smell the wet dirt and blossoming jacaranda trees. The thing that gripped my heart was to read of her spiritual journey through the years and how God carried them. People who read this book will be blessed!"
—JANE FRAY, International Mission Board emeritus missionary and dear friend of Wana Ann

"Dr. Wana Ann Fort shares with us a beautiful, personal view of God's working in the life of a young couple, calling them to serve Him in a challenging place and way. She then insightfully chronicles God's working in the challenges and victories of His committed servants throughout a long and fruitful missionary career. This is a book everyone who cares about missions and missionaries should read."

—CLYDE MEADOR, executive vice-president,
International Mission Board of the Southern Baptist Convention

"I was touched so deeply by Dr. Fort's story. As an aspiring medical missionary, it pulled at many of my heartstrings. If anything, I just wish that I could sit and talk with her. What an incredible life! There is so much spiritual worth in her testimony, and I finished her story with a heavy sense of honor and blessing to 'experience' it through written word."

—ELIZABETH BOURNE, medical student at
Edward Via College of Osteopathic Medicine

"As you turn the pages of this fascinating book, you will travel to rural Africa as Dr. Wana Ann Fort tells her story—a story of faith, compassion, trials, sorrow, joy, and victory. When you come to the final pages, you will thank God for this remarkable missionary doctor whose legacy will live on for generations."

—REBEKAH NAYLOR, MD, emeritus medical missionary and health-care
consultant for Baptist Global Response

"The reality of God, the power of the miraculous, and the adventure of a lifetime are revealed through the never-ending love of two medical missionaries. You will not be able to put this book down until you have taken the journey with Drs. Giles and Wana Ann Fort."

—LEE HALEY, executive pastor, Parkview Baptist Church,
Baton Rouge, Louisiana

"A Thousand Times Yes takes you from laughter to tears and from heartbreak to celebration as Dr. Fort reflects on the challenges, realities, victories, and blessings of meeting both the physical and spiritual needs of people in Africa. It is an extraordinary testimony of what a sovereign God can do through a life that is surrendered to Him and a phenomenal example to the next generation of cross-cultural workers!"

—MELODY HARPER, department chair and assistant professor,
Global Studies Department, Liberty University

A THOUSAND TIMES

YES

A THOUSAND TIMES
YES

Two Doctors
Who Answered God's Call

WANA ANN G. FORT, MD
WITH KIM P. DAVIS

NEW HOPE
PUBLISHERS
Gospel-Centered. Missions-Driven.

BIRMINGHAM, ALABAMA

New Hope® Publishers
P. O. Box 12065
Birmingham, AL 35202-2065
NewHopeDigital.com
New Hope Publishers is a division of WMU®.

Library of Congress Control Number: 2013936962

Thank you to the International Mission Board (IMB) of the Southern Baptist Convention for providing permission to use articles and excerpts about Dr. Wana Ann G. Fort that appeared originally in *The Commission*.

Thank you to: The Ship's List for permission to use information on the SS *Stella Lykes*..

Used by permission of Olan Mills Studios: photo, chapter 14.

Other information regarding historical events and other data concerning Zimbabwe and Malawi are provided through Dr. Wana Ann Fort's letters and notes spanning 60 years, with no intentional violation of any copyright.

Cover designer: Kay Chin Bishop
Interior designer: Glynese Northam
Cover fabric courtesy of: bonsay/shutterstock.com

ISBN-10: 1-59669-383-5
ISBN-13: 978-1-59669-383-8

N134124 · 0813 · 2M1

"For the love of Christ compels us, because we judge thus: that if One died for all, then all died; and He died for all, that those who live should live no longer for themselves, but for Him who died for them and rose again"

(2 CORINTHIANS 5:14–15 NKJV).

Dedication

To my late husband,

the only man I ever loved.
I love you more today than yesterday
but not as much as tomorrow.

Table of Contents

Acknowledgments

When God called me into medical missions, the major drawback was the thought that I would go single, possibly never having a husband or children. God is amazing. He brought a young man in my life who had the same passion for medical missions that I had. Words cannot express my gratitude and love for my late husband, Giles, who passed away on January 14, 2013. We were married for more than 66 years! I miss him dreadfully and can hardly believe he's gone, but I have God's assurance that we will meet again as we worship the Lord Jesus together.

To my five sons, thank you for the delightful years of raising you in Africa and for your attention to me in my senior years. I am proud of you and your families. I am also thankful for the sacrifice made by my parents, my sisters, and Giles's mother and siblings. They were forced to say good-bye many times so that our family could follow God's call. God knew I'd need special parents. Daddy and Mother were amazing parents to me and my six wonderful sisters.

I am thankful for our small church in Harrisonburg, Louisiana, and the first pastor I really remember. I had not become aware of sin in my life until Brother Burton A. Miley came to be our part-time pastor. Finally, I could resist the pull on my heart no longer and surrendered my life to Christ on a Sunday afternoon alone at the church. Later, I discussed with Brother Miley that I felt God had a special plan for me, but I did not know what. He said that God would reveal His plan at the right time and to keep praying.

I am grateful for Sunday School teachers, Training Union (later Discipleship Training) leaders, and GA (Girls' Auxiliary; later known as Girls in Action® [GA®]) leaders who taught the Bible, how to speak, and missions—the three-legged stool, as we called it. I will also never forget Virginia Wingo, my missions mentor. I am thankful for camps and assemblies and for the many churches who prayed for us. To all of you who continue to pray, thank you.

God blessed Giles and me abundantly with many African friends and co-workers. I especially enjoyed WMU®, whether meeting in church buildings or under the trees. In Africa, the WMU women loved their uniforms and worked hard to pass the steps required to wear one. I also worked with older GA groups and Baptist Convention of Zimbabwe leaders; some of my fondest memories are with these brothers and sisters. I will always be grateful for each of our many national brothers and sisters who accepted, loved, and nurtured us.

Our missionary colleagues throughout the years have been like family. I especially thank each one with whom we were privileged to serve. My dear husband often reminded me that I am too verbose, and I know this trait was annoying at times to my missionary friends! Thank you for tolerating my faults. I trust I have been forgiven when I failed you. Each of you is a blessing to me and contributed to who I am today. I appreciate your encouragement to tell my story in a book and if I left your name out of this book, please know this is unintentional. I tried to mention those who came to Zimbabwe between 1952 and the mid-1970s.

My thanks go to New Hope Publishers and WMU for believing in me and making this book possible. I can't begin to thank Kim Davis adequately for using her incredible gifts and many hours of time to write my story. She has been amazingly patient, as my husband died while we were in the book project process. She understood my story since she was a missionary in Zimbabwe as well.

Finally, I want to thank the Lord for calling me to Himself. Wana Ann is an insignificant nobody whom God has chosen to use to honor His holy name. He is the reason for this story.

"Way more than once we were asked, 'Do you really like living in Africa?' I did not have to think about my answer. It was always a thousand times, 'Yes!'"

— WANA ANN G. FORT, MD

Prologue

The blessed smell of rain was in the air, even in the dark clinic made of mud and thin, wooden poles. Seasonal showers had come a few days before and with it the hope of new life and food for the African tribes situated on the Sanyati Reserve. Acacia trees were green, their thorns piercing to the touch by humans, but a sanctuary for the likes of the chirping lilac-breasted roller that commonly found shelter from the downpour in the dense branches.

Ralph Bowlin was not paying attention to the birds or trees or even the rain for that matter. In fact, since coming to Southern Rhodesia (Zimbabwe) a few months earlier, he had no time to sit and enjoy nature. There were too many other pressing needs such as the newly opened mission school, the constant influx of people's requests, malaria, snakes, and basic survival. The stress and difficulties were enough to cause even a devoted missionary to question his sanity in bringing his wife to this remote part of Africa. Yet, the compassion felt when he saw the desperate need of the people for the truth of the gospel compelled him to put aside any question of his calling from God. Thus, when he was interrupted by an urgent cry, he left what he was doing to see who was causing the racket.

"*Mufundisi, mufundisi*," the African called for the missionary without delay as he neared the two-room hut. Bowlin peered through the doorway to find a young man out of breath and completely soaked. Other men and women who helped on the station, as well as a few children, came to see the purpose of the summons, their curiosity aroused. Bowlin approached the man outside, greeting him with elementary *Shona* phrases. With the help of others, the messenger communicated that a young woman was very ill near Chief Neuso's village. Because the rain had been heavy, the man had to swim across the swollen river ten miles away and then walk to get to the new mission station. He was half-starved and exhausted.

About that time, Bowlin's wife, Betty, emerged to see the commotion for herself. In no time, the couple and the man got in the truck and took the muddy path through the bush. It was not easy due to the weather, and frankly Bowlin didn't know if they'd even make it to the river.

Finally, he maneuvered the vehicle to the water's edge and stopped the engine. He had no idea how they would cross the currents, much less bring back the one who needed medical attention. There was no choice but to take the crude *machilla* (stretcher) and wade across.

For two days, a sweat-drenched woman had been in the birthing hut as several of the old *ambuyas* (grandmothers) made clucking noises with their tongues, somberly attending to her. She was spread out on an old cloth on the dirt floor. The smell of smoke permeated the enclosure where a small fire was the only light in the dark space. In half-conscious agony, the woman was in bad condition as her mother wailed and carried on beside her. The baby would not come out.

Upon the men's arrival to the village on the other side of the river, the patient was carefully loaded onto the stretcher. Then the trek began back to the river as the villagers followed. To cross the currents, the men had to hold their burden above their heads in the deepest part of the water.

When Betty and Ralph assessed the dire situation, they knew the woman and baby's only chance of survival was for Bowlin to take her to the hospital in Gatooma (Kadoma), 60 miles away. Still on the stretcher, she was placed in the back of the truck. They made their way to the station to gather a few supplies for the trip, supplies such as food and shovels for when the truck would get stuck.

Provisions were packed, including sandwiches and water since it would take several hours into the night to get to Gatooma. As the woman moaned in the back of the truck, the Africans who had quietly gathered around could only sigh and shake their heads, knowing that she probably would not make it, the plight of so many of their young women during childbirth.

Bowlin drove slowly on the washed-out road, if one could call it a road. Several times the truck got stuck, and the African men who rode with him helped to repeatedly dig the tires out of the muck. Halfway there, however, hope completely faded when the truck slid off the crude road and into a ditch, bogging down right up to the axle. After much effort of digging and trying to free the truck in the dark night, it was no use. As soon as the sun rose, Bowlin sent a man on a bicycle to find and bring back his colleague, Clyde Dotson, who lived in Gatooma. All Bowlin could do was gingerly bring the woman on the stretcher to the ground and attempt to help her himself.

After being notified and a day and night of trying to get his vehicle through the mud, Clyde Dotson finally located the roadside camp at dawn on the third day of the ordeal. What Dotson found was heartbreaking. The young missionary, whom Dotson had recruited in the States, was sitting by the roadside—dirty, dehydrated, and hungry. The sandwiches and water had run out two days before. But worse, a few feet away lay the lifeless bodies of a young woman and a half-born baby. Bowlin was despondent and on the verge of collapse.

Bowlin tearfully told the senior missionary the whole story. "If only there had been medical help, she might have lived," he sobbed. Together, they dug a grave by the side of the road and then knelt on the ground. Knowing that the woman had probably not heard the name of Jesus and seeing the desperate need of the people they had come to love, they cried out in anguish to the Lord that He would send them a doctor and provide a hospital on the Sanyati Reserve. Then reverently, the mud was shoveled into the grave, marking the desperate prayer of two missionaries.

The Realness of the Lord

"NOTHING GOOD EVER comes out of Catahoula Hills!" This declaration was the popular opinion of my father's relatives, which they expressed after he set up his law practice in Harrisonburg, Louisiana. Being the oldest child of David Wanamaker and Izetta Gibson, I was puzzled why anyone would say such a thing. I suppose my relatives honestly believed that my father or his children would never amount to much if we lived in such a place. To my father's credit, he didn't let the extended family change our geography.

Harrisonburg, in those days, was just a village in Catahoula Parish situated on the Ouachita River, quite a distance from big cities like New Orleans or Baton Rouge. It had been the ancient ground of Native American settlements and later nearby Fort Beauregard. The courthouse was in the middle of Harrisonburg, the parish seat, and we also had a school, a drugstore, a few other businesses, a post office, the Baptist church, and the Methodist church. We lived in a big, white house across the road from the courthouse and about two blocks from the river bridge. Even to this day, if you blink while driving through, you might miss Harrisonburg. It was home, however, and I wouldn't have wanted to grow up anywhere else.

At my birth in June 1924, my mother named me after my father. She had hoped I would be a boy. She decided not to name me David, but rather passed on part of his middle name. When my father was born in 1889, my grandfather, David Hewitt Gibson, named my father after himself and the famous Wanamakers of New England. Grandpa and Grandma Gibson had a penchant to give their numerous children unique names such as Juan Alfonso (which they pronounced JU-an, with a hard J sound), Lizzie Jermena, Letha Maleta, Lenora Pieta, and Lettia Eulala, to name just a few. Perhaps the shortened version of Wana was a blessing rather than having the name Jermena or Eulala.

My dad rarely called me Wana Ann. Most of the time, it was just Anner. It often got a little confusing since he was referred to as Wannie. My mom was known as Zeckie to most people, but when I was first talking, I called her MeMe. Nicknames stuck in our family.

MeMe was Baptist to the bone. Her Baptist ancestor came from England to Rhode Island before the Revolutionary War and founded the first Baptist church there before returning to England. Other family members came later. A long line of Baptist preachers were in her family, including my maternal grandfather who was an itinerant preacher. She loved church, although my father was a nominal Baptist at best. He attended with my mother until he got mad at a visiting revival preacher one Sunday. I was only two years old, but somehow I sneaked out of the pew where my parents sat and crept up to the pulpit platform where all the action was taking place. My parents' eyes were huge as saucers when they saw me walking around behind the preacher while he was preaching. When the reverend heard the giggles and saw me taking the attention away from his sermon, he proceeded to comment that whoever the parents were of this misbehaved child should come immediately and get her. My daddy marched up to the platform to retrieve his errant daughter and stomped back up the aisle toward the back of the sanctuary, not stopping until he reached home, a block away. My mother hardly could keep up with him. That was the final nail in the coffin of my father's consistent church days. Regardless of the humiliation, however, MeMe swallowed her pride and decided forgiveness was the high road. She made sure that I—and the sisters after me—would be in church every time the doors were open.

Even though my dad wasn't religious, he was a good and decent man, well respected in the community. He often had visits from the residents and always welcomed people of every skin color. He'd show a family into the parlor and ask me to serve refreshments. I'd come back in with a plate of cookies and something to drink, and I'd hear him say, "Son, you made a mistake." My father proceeded to tell a young man in trouble to get his life straightened out, but he'd represent him fairly. Being a country lawyer had its challenges, particularly financial. Most people who needed his services were poor, and even though he had a law degree from Louisiana State University, he didn't bring in a lot of money. He was paid much of the time in slabs of bacon, eggs, and vegetables. We were well fed but financially strained.

When I was two, MeMe gave birth to a son, but the labor was difficult and my baby brother didn't survive. My parents kept trying to have a boy but finally stopped after having seven girls. My daddy said that he was the only man in Louisiana who lived with eight women. My mom eventually had to find a job as the district registrar of voters to help support the family during the years of the Great Depression. I can remember going to the store as a young teenager with a short list of groceries to purchase, and the owner, Mr. Beasley, would say, "See if you can pay a little somethin' on the account this week." I'd leave the store wanting to crawl under a rock.

MeMe probably contributed as much to my learning as my father did, outside of school. She had taken some college courses and always encouraged me to learn. She was nine years younger than my daddy. There wasn't anything she couldn't cook. No one could make a rhubarb-apple pie like she could. It was pink inside with a delicate, flaky crust. Because we couldn't get rhubarb locally, my daddy was known to drive all the way to New Orleans to buy some when he was on a business trip to Baton Rouge. We had a woodstove, and while I watched her cook as she sang hymns, a sense of joy was present amidst the delicious smells and laughter. If she wasn't singing, she was quoting poetry. I remember sitting on the front porch when an old schoolteacher and MeMe would take turns reading poems as my sisters and I sat entranced by the beauty of the verses. As the pungent smell of Mother's rose bushes permeated the air, the rhythmic words sounded like music on that porch.

Daddy used to love to hear Mother sing too. Almost every Sunday afternoon, he'd pile his girls in the car and take a Sunday afternoon drive. We'd ride with no real destination that I knew of, and he'd tell us girls to be quiet while MeMe sang. He'd say, "MeMe, sing 'Red Sails in the Sunset.'" It was a popular doo-wop tune on the radio in the mid-1930s, lyrics written by Jimmy Kennedy. She'd smile and begin crooning in her rich voice, "Red sails in the sunset, way out on the sea; Oh, carry my loved one home safely to me." Her voice would lull the little sisters to sleep, and I would sit there in the backseat and wish I could sing like that. Then she'd jump into another song with Kennedy lyrics, "Isle of Capri." She could sing all vocal parts in perfect pitch, but she particularly had a beautiful alto voice. Her singing would go on and on until my father finally turned the car around and headed home.

Even though my dad didn't have a living son, he didn't let that deter him from passing on his fishing skills. My sisters and I learned to snag a fish, and I caught many as any girl, wading almost shoulder-deep to catch them and gutting and cleaning them later. Fishing was how my father escaped from the stress of life, I guess. We girls didn't mind, because we got to spend quality time with our daddy.

Chapter 1

As much as I loved my family, I couldn't wait to go to school each day. I loved every subject. Often, my teachers gave me extra schoolbooks because I would get way ahead of the class. I was particularly good at math, and I also loved to write. Once I wrote a creative story about being snake-bitten (of course, it was imaginary) and won a prize. Reading was my favorite pastime. Since our school library was small, I think I read every single book there. When a new book came in, it felt like Christmas. I wanted to be the first to read each new title. The classics, biographies, history—you name it, I read it. All those books encouraged my imagination. Being the oldest of seven daughters, I organized my sisters to play school, explore an enchanted forest, or pretend a fallen tree in our yard was a pirate ship and we were the pirates! There was never a dull moment.

Mother never did care much for discipline, and perhaps that's why I had been found up at the front of the church as a young child, but I always felt loved by her. She was profoundly happy. She loved to be with people. After school, MeMe would take her "hour" to visit with friends. I'd babysit and supervise the chores, which was mostly sweeping, while she'd run down to the drugstore to drink a soda and catch up on the local news. I'd get upset with one of my sisters, who claimed to have a headache most days to get out of her work. But I knew MeMe probably wouldn't do anything about it. Resentment built up in my heart toward my sister. By the time I was 12 years old, God was knocking on the door of that same heart. Sunday School, Training Union, Girls' Auxiliary (or GA; later known as Girls in Action® [GA®])—you name it, I was involved at church. But deep down, I was feeling guilty. I felt so guilty about my selfishness after church one April Sunday that I left my house in the middle of a marble game with friends and ran to the church. Going inside the empty sanctuary, I crawled behind the piano and fell on my face. I didn't want anyone to see me. Feeling God's presence, I confessed my bitterness toward my sister and everything else I could think of and asked Jesus to take control of my life. I thanked Him for loving me and for His death on the Cross to save me. I rose up, wiped my tear-stained face, and had a lighter step on the way home. Later that night, I shared my experience with our church congregation. When the weather warmed up, I was baptized at Bird's Creek, just a few miles from our church.

About a year or two later, I was up late one night reading in my room. I shared a room with Evelyn, who was two when Mother's last baby, Rose Katherine, was born. I sort of "took over" Evelyn at that time. She never complained when I kept the light on for a while. There was always a good book to read. That particular night I was reading after strategically placing a blanket over the crack under the door so my mother wouldn't know I was still up. The house was quiet as I finished the story about a poor family who lived in the Ozark Mountains in Arkansas. I couldn't believe how they lived, and it struck me that God had designed my destiny. I could have been born in those Arkansas hills, but I wasn't. In fact, I had nothing to do with who I was, where I was born, or who my parents were. All was determined by God, who loved the world, even Wana Ann Gibson.

I crept to the sunroom off my bedroom and stared up into the dark sky filled with a myriad of bright stars. "When I consider thy heavens, the work of thy fingers, the moon and the stars, which thou hast ordained; What is man, that Thou art mindful of him? and the son of man, that thou visitest him?" (Psalm 8:3–4 KJV). I was nearly overcome by the awareness of His presence. Peering toward Widow Stone's yard across the street and just above a big cedar tree, I saw the North Star, looking like a diamond in the sky. Then I observed the Big Dipper. That's when I realized that God had blessed me for a purpose. He had every right to claim all of my life. I didn't know what His will for me was, but I knew it would be helping others. That night, I gave Him my life to do His will.

There were three women at our church who served as teachers for GA, a missions organization for girls created by Woman's Missionary Union® (WMU®), Auxiliary to Southern Baptist Convention, and largest Protestant missions organization for women in the world. Mrs. Hill, Mrs. Neal, and Mrs. Girlinghouse introduced me to continents such as Africa and Asia in a whole, new perspective: missions. GA to me wasn't only completing the various work requirements called Forward Steps from Maiden to Queen Regent, but it instructed me about prayer, Bible study, giving, and sharing the gospel. I was also confronted with horizons that I didn't know existed. Each summer there was a five-day GA camp for teenagers between the ages of 13 and 16. At the first GA summer camp I attended when I was 14, I met Virginia Wingo, a state GA leader. My friend Grace and I enjoyed hearing the experiences of a South American missionary; heartstrings were being tugged. We were also looking forward to the scavenger hunt and to my great surprise, I won and was presented the prize of a watermelon by Miss Wingo. That evening after supper enough watermelons were brought out for everyone to enjoy, which was quite a treat.

One night at camp, I sensed the Holy Spirit's presence so deeply that I had to excuse myself and go into an empty room at the camp. I got down on my knees, and the realness of the Lord rolled over me like the waves of the sea. After a few minutes, I came out of the room. The session had closed. One of the camp teachers asked me to talk to a girl who was a not a Christian. We began to talk, and before I knew it, I was sharing my salvation story. The girl knew that night that she wanted to commit her life to Jesus too, so she prayed with me and accepted God's grace. It was thrilling to have a part in her decision. On the last night of camp, I was astounded when I was elected to be the Star GA Camper and given a special pen. However, that didn't compare to seeing a fellow camper come to Christ.

The next day, my parents were a little late to pick me up, and I had a good talk with Miss Wingo. She encouraged me to continue in GA as a leader. Over the next few years, Miss Wingo mentored me through letters and the times I would see her at summer camp. Through her influence, God began to work in my heart about missions. She would always tell me not to worry about God's will because He would lead me each step of the way and when it was time, He'd reveal His plan for my life. Psalm 37:5 became my favorite verse: "Commit your way to the LORD, Trust also in Him, And He shall bring it to pass."

High school gave me the opportunity to devour new knowledge. A favorite class was home economics taught by Miss Shirley Wren. My freshman year, Miss Wren chose five students to represent our school at the Louisiana State Fair, and I was one of those who got to present and discuss the features of an ideal kitchen. Later, Miss Wren nominated me to be the president of the Louisiana Junior Homemaker's Club. Each nominee had to give a speech, and I was elected. It was an exciting time! Being president gave me the chance to go to Cleveland for the National Homemaker's Convention. At 16, I rode a train all the way to Ohio by myself. Because I was representing Louisiana, a woman from the state office taught me how to walk on to a stage. I'm afraid she thought because I was from Harrisonburg, I might embarrass the state! I gave the Louisiana state report and participated in a panel discussion.

As my happy days of high school were coming to a close, the world seemed to be falling apart. Even in our little spot on earth, we heard about Germany's invasion of Poland and the declaration of war by Britain and France. Gathering around the radio, we heard the Fireside Chats of President Roosevelt become more serious. What involvement might America have in the war and would that affect me? Packing my trunks to take to Louisiana Polytechnic Institute (Louisiana Tech) as a freshman, I had no idea how World War II would indeed change my life forever.

CHAPTER 2

A Whisper in My Ear

WHEN MY DADDY pulled into the circle in front of the freshman girls dorm at Louisiana Tech in Ruston, I thought I had died and gone to heaven. I know it sounds eccentric, but learning was my favorite thing in the world to experience. The opening of the fall semester had been postponed a month due to army maneuvers in the area, so classes began in October 1941. Thankfully, gas rationing had not started yet, so this time Daddy drove me the 112 miles from our country town to the big city.

A young student wearing a sweater with a big *T* on the front was selling license tags in the circle in front of the dorm. Dad pulled up beside him and, with a marked country drawl adopted especially for the occasion, asked, "Is there any place around here where we can stop and eat our cold biscuits and bacon for lunch? I've brought my daughter here to go to college, but we need to eat before I leave her."

I guess I should have been mortified, but his joking relieved the tension as we laughed together, to the confusion of the student who just stared at us like we had three horns. I could tell my father was trying to make things lighthearted so that I wouldn't get emotional, but I knew he was struggling to leave me there. All too soon we were saying good-byes at the front door. "Anner, you write your mama and take care of yourself," he said as he hugged me good-bye. I watched the car disappear around a curve. The big lump in my throat slowly dissolved as I went bounding up the stairs to begin the fun and excitement of college life.

I loved every subject. In fact, because I was fascinated with every class, I had no idea what to choose as a major. My mind was like a sponge, and I couldn't get enough. But it wasn't only the studies, it was also the campus activities. There was something to do every minute of the day and not enough hours to do everything.

But before I could get one semester under my belt, the Japanese attacked Pearl Harbor. President Roosevelt declared in his speech that December 7, 1941, was "a date which will live in infamy." Some of the male students on campus immediately signed up for military service, while others who were seniors tried to hold out until graduation. It was an unsettling time as we began to see how World War II would change our lives.

When it was time for graduation exercises in May 1942, another freshman and I sat in the balcony near the front row in Howard Auditorium. Watching as diplomas were awarded gave me goose bumps. The school of engineering was being recognized when the dean called the name of a tall, slightly stooped young man and added "summa cum laude." He was the only one in the class that night to graduate with highest honors. The audience began to applaud loudly as he shook hands with the college president and took his diploma. I thought, *When I graduate, I am going to get my degree summa cum laude.*

Besides fear, the biggest change due to the war was the lack of male students during my sophomore year. There were certainly no distractions! I immersed myself in more campus activities, including leadership roles at the Baptist Student Union (BSU; now Baptist Collegiate Ministry). Before long, I heard about BSU week that would be held in the coming summer at Ridgecrest Baptist Conference Center (now LifeWay Conference Center at Ridgecrest) near Asheville, North Carolina. There was nothing I wanted to do more than attend. So I started praying, because I knew it would take a lot to persuade my father that I needed to go. Not only that, it cost 15 dollars, not counting my travel expenses. I had to come up with a convincing plan. Putting my brain to work, I entered an essay contest and won, receiving 5 dollars as the prize. Then I gave a speech and was paid 10 dollars. With this money in hand, I went to my dad and told him all about the camp. With my dad thinking

I was a little too fanatical about my religion, he wasn't keen on the idea. After more convincing, he finally agreed that I could go and provided the additional money needed. A friend and I went to Ridgecrest together. We couldn't believe how nice the rooms were! Anticipation was high for what God might do in my life, and I was ready. At the very start of the week, I walked up to the prayer garden alone and asked God to show me His will for my life. I still had not declared a major, I was not dating, and basically, I didn't know where my life was headed. On Sunday morning while there, I was sitting in a Sunday School class when all of a sudden, I heard a voice in my right ear whisper, "Wana Ann, you are going to be a medical missionary." It was so real that I looked around the room to see if other people had heard the voice. Instead of listening to the lesson, I began rationalizing in my mind with God. I told God He was talking to the wrong person.

As soon as lunch was over, I quickly walked up the hill to the prayer garden and in earnest told God why I could not be a medical missionary. If anyone passed by, I would have been a sight to see! I didn't even reverently pray—I ranted. "God, You have made a mistake. Don't you know women do not go to medical school? My daddy won't want me to be a doctor. I'll be a missionary teacher or nurse or anything else! And don't you know that I do not want to be a single missionary? It would be impossible!" But just like Jonah, I didn't get anywhere with Him. After three days of agonizing over it, I was exhausted and submitted to do His will *if* He would be with me each step. And I told Him that He'd have to do it through me because I certainly could not do it otherwise.

I came home from Ridgecrest not knowing what to say to my father, so I talked to MeMe first. She listened to me and was supportive. She must have known it would be harder to tell Daddy. Maybe she gently prepared him; I'm not sure. When I got up enough nerve to approach my father, he was sitting on the back porch reading *Newsweek*. He read two newspapers a day and stayed up on world events. I was so afraid to tell him about wanting to be a medical missionary that I couldn't even face him. So I tiptoed up behind him and said hurriedly before I lost my courage, "Daddy, I am going to be a medical missionary." The statement hung in the air for a few moments until he finally asked me, "Anner, can't you be a missionary without being a doctor?" I told him that I wouldn't consider any other profession.

As the war escalated, Louisiana Tech was selected to participate in the US government's V-12 Navy College Training Program to train navy and marine servicemen. On July 1, 1943, we would change to a trimester program, thus I would begin my junior year two months early. When we heard this news about the V-12s, we college girls were quite excited at the prospect of having more men on campus again—and men in uniforms too!

I had a difficult time scheduling all the science courses I needed for my newly declared major in biology and minor in chemistry. There would be many required courses for entrance into medical school. Still remembering the voice of

God, I would not be deterred. I prayed even harder for God's will to be accomplished. When some of my friends heard of my commitment to missions, I was asked to give a testimony at a state BSU event. After it was over, I heard that some of the student leaders laughed behind my back saying that I would never be a medical missionary. They even made fun of my BSU directors for asking me to share my testimony. I knew though since God had called me to medical missions, He would see it happen.

The science courses were overwhelming. If I thought I had studied before, it was multiplied by 100. I had a heavy schedule with long hours in the lab. Not only that, but I had a part-time job in the speech department helping with stage sets and theater productions and assisting the speech teacher. Of course, I was still involved in BSU, campus academic organizations, and the First Baptist Church of Ruston where I taught Sunday School to teenage girls. My freshman goal never wavered either: summa cum laude.

The scariest thing, however, was the thought that since God had called me to be a medical missionary, I might have to be single for the rest of my life. But God had a surprise for me. When the V-12 participants came to Louisiana Tech, the BSU invited these young commissioned officers to come to a welcome party, which I was responsible for as the social chairman. A large crowd attended. We invited anyone who had served on the BSU council in his college to attend our BSU Greater Council meeting the next afternoon. At the council meeting, we sat down in a circle, with the only empty chair next to me. A young man came in late and sat down. Before the meeting dismissed, we paired up with the person beside us to pray. That was the first time I met Milton Giles Fort Jr. He was so cute that I couldn't believe my good fortune! He told me that he graduated from Texas A&M and was going to be a medical missionary. Before long, I was telling him my story and that God had also called me to be a missionary doctor. With a grin on his face, he said, "Well, even an Aggie can figure this out!" We only had eyes for each other, and a few months later on our way to church, he told me he loved me. I loved him too. He gave me a kiss—my first kiss. We went in the church building to Sunday School; but before church, he slipped me into an empty room and stole another kiss. Thankfully, nobody saw!

I was still a student at Louisiana Tech, and Giles had commitments with the navy before attending medical school. His V-12 group was sent to midshipman's training in New York near one of the lakes. It was icy cold, and he had to shovel snow at the officer training school. Giles became ill for two weeks. When his shoveling responsibilities resumed, he had a relapse. The course lasted three months, and he missed at least four weeks from illness. I was afraid he might not pass the course. However, the navy needed officers to prepare for invading Japan, so they didn't fail him. He was shipped to Florida for small boat training to land on beaches. About 14 men would go out in a boat and land it precisely on shore. Timing the boat landing with the tides was essential. They trained all summer long.

While Giles was preparing to go to Japan, I graduated from Tech in an accelerated graduation ceremony due to the war. October 18, 1944, was my big day because by the grace of God, I was graduating summa cum laude. My parents had used precious rationed gasoline to make the trip and were already seated to see me awarded a Bachelor of Science in biology and chemistry.

Our class solemnly marched to our places, resplendent in black cap and gown. At the scheduled time, my dean, Dr. Hughes, came forward to call his roster of names. Somehow, the students were all crowded together by the platform steps, and the dean was having difficulty keeping his place as he looked at each student, calling out the name. One by one, the graduates were presented; then it was my turn. He looked at me with recognition in his eyes and announced, "Miss Wana Ann Gibson, uh . . . magna cum laude." He mistakenly announced the wrong accomplishment! I was crushed. I was the only graduate to receive summa cum laude that day, but it wasn't even announced. My parents were disappointed, and the dean and everyone else probably never knew he made the mistake. I went back to my seat incredulous.

After it sunk in, I couldn't help chuckling to myself over the irony of it all. With God's help, I had dreamed, persevered, studied, and worked. My goal had been accomplished, even though unaccompanied by the recognition I desired. Right there on my "sheepskin" in front of me, the words were forever engraved, *summa cum laude*, but God dealt with my pride that day.

Straight from graduation, I got involved in the war effort by working in a bullet factory laboratory halfway between Ruston and Shreveport. Certifying the weight, size, and density of the material for the bullets was not exactly medical work, but it paid 90 cents an hour. I needed the money for medical school. My father, who had opposed my decision to be a missionary doctor, had not offered financial assistance for my additional schooling. My sights were set on Baylor Medical School, and no one told me it would be hard to get in. I thought you just applied and went! Since Giles wanted to go to Baylor after serving his country, I assumed Baylor was my only option.

Before Giles headed for training in Panama and the Philippines, his ship docked in Mississippi. Giles let me know, and I took the jam-packed bus to Jackson so that I could see him. (Buses were incredibly overcrowded due to gasoline rationing during the war.) How wonderful it was to meet him at the station! We walked around town, got a meal, and then sat up all night at the station, making promises of marriage and commitment. We prayed for the war to be over soon so that we could be together again. I thought my heart would break when I had to say good-bye before he returned to his ship the next afternoon. I begged God to protect Giles more times than I could possibly count. A few months later when word came that the atom bomb had been dropped twice on cities in Japan, the ship Giles was on went straight to that island country. Before they could get there, Japan surrendered on August 15, 1945. Giles and the other sailors would not have to invade Japan! He literally got off the ship onto Japanese soil and went souvenir shopping, buying two clay pots! After that, he was put on a list to be discharged as soon as he had enough service points.

When the war came to a close in the summer of 1945, my job at the bullet factory immediately ended. I was able to get another job in Shreveport, working for a doctor who needed help with lab work and taking x-rays. While working there, I wrote to Baylor College of Medicine in Houston, Texas, asking for an application. I received a letter back that stated since half the class was serving in the military, they were not taking students from out of state. Well, I wasn't summa cum laude for nothing, and there was no way that I would take no for an answer. So I wrote them back and said I that I had graduated at the top of my class at Louisiana Tech and simply had to get into medical school. I was very naive and thought that if one wanted to go to medical school, he or she could choose one and go. I only applied to Baylor. I took my tests and got references. God must have intervened despite my naïveté, because I was notified that I would not even have to come for an interview. They accepted me.

I packed up and headed to medical school the fall of 1945. Not knowing when Giles and I would be able to get married, I concentrated on my studies. I was one of five girls in my anatomy class. I loved everything I learned and was committed to making all As, which I did my first year. Another female medical student, Annabeth Connell, and

I became fast friends and stuck together as we invaded this man's world, full steam ahead.

At last, word came that Giles would be coming home! We began making plans to get married as soon as we could and set the date for Friday, June 14, 1946, at the Harrisonburg Baptist Church. Giles's mother, Alma, was a widow and had been since Giles was a toddler. His father had passed away due to tuberculosis that he had contracted while serving as a pharmacist in the military. A devoted follower of the Lord, Giles's father sensed God was calling him to be a pastor, so he uprooted his young family (which at that time was Giles's mother, Giles's older sister, and two-year-old Giles) and enrolled at Southwestern Baptist Theological Seminary. But he would never see graduation since he died suddenly from complications of tuberculosis. Giles's little brother was born a few months after his father's death. Mrs. Fort was a woman of fortitude, no doubt, and raised three children with the help of her mother. When Giles discussed with his "Ami" about getting married, she was at first opposed. She was afraid the financial strains of both of us being in medical school would keep Giles from finishing his degree. I wrote a letter to this godly woman and promised he would graduate, even if I had to drop out temporarily and work to support him. She decided to come to our wedding. My father walked me down the aisle as I carried a white Bible and a bouquet of white orchids and carnations. That Friday evening, I married the only man I had ever loved or kissed.

We cashed in some service stamps that we had purchased to pay part of my second-year medical school bills. Giles was accepted at Baylor and was just one year behind me. Contacting the Southern Baptist Foreign Mission Board (FMB; now International Mission Board), we applied for the program that they had in the 1940s that would give some financial assistance for medical school if we committed to being missionaries. So with the FMB's help, an externship for Giles at Methodist and Montrose hospitals, and good summer jobs, we managed to get through medical school while actively serving in Second Baptist Church of Houston, being in honors societies or medical fraternities, and being in leadership roles at the state level and medical school's BSU. Giles even pastored a small Baptist church in the area.

Finally, my graduation date from Baylor College of Medicine came. I was one of three women in a class of 62 graduates in 1949. That day I thought of how God had whispered in my ear that I would be a medical missionary and that He had enabled me to follow through with what He had called me to do. Our third wedding anniversary was one day after I graduated with honors and became Dr. Wana Ann G. Fort. Giles joked that for a year he'd have to put up with letters addressed to Mr. and Dr. Fort! He was always the jokester.

While Giles finished his last year of medical school, my first year as a doctor was as an assistant in pediatrics at Jefferson Davis Hospital in Houston. I got paid 25 dollars per month with free lodging, meals, and laundry service. We were thrilled! After Giles graduated, he became an intern at Jefferson Davis Hospital, and I became a resident physician there and at Hermann Hospital. Eventually, Giles became a resident physician at Jefferson Davis. We were getting closer and closer to our goal of being able to leave for missionary service.

It was bound to happen, but after nearly six years of marriage and nearly completing the requirements to pursue missions, we had our first baby boy on April 24, 1952—Milton Giles Fort III, whom we affectionately called Gilesie. I was nearly 28 years old, much older than most women having their first baby in the 1950s. I looked at our beautiful firstborn and prayed the Lord would protect him from harm wherever our future overseas might lead. Communists had closed China as a missions field, the place Giles always thought he'd end up, so we knew we wouldn't be going there. It was about this time that we heard a heartbreaking story from a missionary speaker named Clyde Dotson.

CHAPTER 3

A Tug on Our Hearts

AFTER THE TRAGIC and distressing deaths of the mother and stillborn infant along the side of the road, Ralph Bowlin was even more determined to pray for a doctor to come and help. Clyde Dotson and his wife, Hattie, left for a short furlough (now stateside assignment) to the States and promised to spread the news of how urgently a doctor was needed at the newly acquired mission station in Southern Rhodesia's Sanyati Reserve.

Bowlin himself had heard the impassioned missionary speak in the late 1940s as Mr. Dotson shared how he went out to the Rimuka Township on a Sunday morning, looking for an opportunity to preach. When he saw a group of men sitting under a tree drinking homemade beer, he began singing a Ndau hymn. Claiming that he borrowed the congregation under the tree from the devil, he and two or three African brothers went back each week to preach and share Christ. People began repenting. Bowlin's heart was touched. When he discovered that the Dotsons, veteran missionaries with another organization for nearly 20 years, had been contracted by the Southern Baptist Foreign Mission Board (FMB; now International Mission Board) in 1950 as pioneer missionaries in Southern Rhodesia, Bowlin contacted the Virginia-based organization. He and Betty had been in the process with the FMB and asked to be sent to Southern Rhodesia to be on Dotson's team. The Bowlins were appointed December 7, 1950, arriving in Gatooma seven months later. The Dotsons then moved out to the government-donated mission station of Sanyati Reserve, awarded to Southern Baptists who promised to open a school and medical facility for the people living there. With their four youngest children, the Dotsons set up camp for months under the trees. A clinic of poles and mud was built, and a piece of tin was nailed to a tree for a blackboard at the outdoor school. Hattie knew a little first aid, and people began coming. The prayer for a doctor became more and more urgent.

Then the Bowlins and Dotsons switched locations so that the Dotsons could prepare to go on furlough. Mr. Dotson promised to recruit a doctor. Betty became the principal of the school at Sanyati. They lived in a hut while a modest house was being built. The two-room clinic also served as a kitchen and bath for them, and a seven-room building had been completed for the school. Village schools were also started, one where Chief Neuso lived, a new believer in Christ. Bowlin preached on Sundays at the village schools. More and more, Bowlin saw people who were dying needlessly due to poor birthing methods, malaria, malnutrition, and other maladies. Besides that, he and Betty might need a doctor, too, if *they* were snake-bitten! Already he shot one or two cobras a day, once in their bedroom. Most distressing was the death of the mother and child on the side of the road before the Dotsons went on furlough.

The opening of Baptist work in the Sanyati Reserve and Southern Rhodesia was happening as we were finishing up our medical training. Having started the application process with the FMB for missionary service, we began looking for the place God had chosen for us. In a letter from the FMB, we were asked to consider pioneer medical missions work in Southern Rhodesia. Knowing little about that country, we began to study some geography and pray, but somehow we felt even as we first read the letter that this was the place. Once again, I wasn't too happy about God's will. I didn't really want to go to an isolated, rural bush station 60 miles from town over a trail cut through the bush—a trail that was nearly impassable in the rainy season and very rough in the dry season. I really did not want to live where there was no electricity, no dependable water supply, no other doctor to take care of our beautiful son, no grocery store, and no telephone. I didn't want to even think about snakes, wild animals, or deadly mosquitoes!

We were able to meet Clyde Dotson while he was in the States. He told us story after story of what was going on in this wild and remote area in Africa. He described how people were coming to Christ, but he didn't sugarcoat the difficulties. He mentioned how the Bowlins killed snakes and that leopards and lions were often spotted in the area. I began shaking when he asked Giles if he owned a rifle and knew how to shoot. I didn't hesitate to say that I didn't know a thing about shooting! The clincher, however, was hearing a story of a young mother and her unborn baby who died on the side of the road as another missionary tried to get her to the only hospital, 60 miles away. I felt as though God reached down and touched my heart. And I couldn't ignore the fact that Giles had that look on his face that said, "This is for me!" Deep down, I was reluctantly drawn to Sanyati too.

Again, I came to the place in prayer that I could tell the Lord this was impossible for me to do, but I would commit my way to Him, trusting in Him to bring it all to pass for His honor. How marvelous it is that God knows the best way for His children! Giles and I prayed about it and told the personnel at the FMB that we felt called to meet the challenge through the power of His Spirit at work in us. And then we ordered a couple of .22-caliber pistols! I even went up to Fort Hill in my home town of Harrisonburg to practice shooting.

During our appointment preliminaries in Richmond in October 1952, we were interviewed by an examining committee. We had answered several questions about our call and training when one person asked my husband, "Dr. Fort, how are you going to manage in a primitive situation like Sanyati? The doctors I know here in Richmond, Virginia, live in beautiful homes in the best sections of town. They have things money can buy to make life comfortable and pleasant. How will you handle that marked difference in income, living conditions, and standards?"

I was glad we had previously faced this question and proud of Giles as he responded, "Sir, Jesus said, 'Life does not consist of the abundance of the things thereof!' And Jesus said, 'If you keep My commandments, you will abide in My love. . . . I have told you these things that My joy may be in you and that your joy may be full.' What He said is true!"

My father, however, was not happy about Giles and me wanting to be medical missionaries, much less going to Africa. By that time, he was a district attorney and an expert in questioning a person and making one feel guilty. He made the case that we were throwing our medical degrees away. My dad, who had always been fair to everyone while representing them, all of a sudden made an appalling statement, "If all you want to do is take care of black folk, there are plenty of them in Louisiana!" MeMe, of course, was supportive of us. I knew she would smooth things over for me with Daddy. Needless to say, it was painful to continue God's call on our lives without my father's blessing.

Giles and I began in earnest to find out everything we could about Southern Rhodesia. We wrote a letter to a doctor in the capital city of Salisbury (Harare) who told us the San-yati Reserve was a lot like West Texas. He had been through there and encouraged us to pursue coming. We researched the history of Rhodesia from books; there was no Google. The original residents were bushmen who lived in caves and left cave paintings. By A.D. 200, the Bantu migrated from West Africa and drove the bushmen from their hunting grounds. Around 1075, an unconfirmed tribe of people built the kingdom of Great Zimbabwe, its stone ruins still visible today. When the Portuguese began trading along the Arab settlements on the eastern coast of Africa, the first of the settlers came to the area of "the Mutapa," the name given to the leader of the Mutapa people. The Mutapa became very rich as he charged taxes to the traders and travelers of his area who came to mine gold and kill elephants for their ivory tusks. Eventually the first Portuguese Jesuit missionary came to visit the Mutapa, and many were converted to Christianity, including the ruler himself. However, the missionary was eventually murdered. Dominicans and Jesuits continued to come over the years, and many tribesmen deserted their beliefs in Mwari, their high god who spoke from different elements of nature, sometimes a human medium, and was said to be the ancestor of the first Changamire, the head of the Rozwi tribe. When more and more Portuguese mercenaries came, the Mutapa and Changamire united together to drive them out. Other tribes settled such as the Nguni, Shangaan, Sotho, Lozi, and Shona. Eventually the Matabele people came, with their famous rulers of Mzilikazi and his son, Lobengula.

It was all a bit overwhelming to learn about a strange and different place, culture, and beliefs when it wasn't just a history lesson. We were actually going to live there. Reading about David Livingstone and his father-in-law, Robert Moffat, and some of their missionary experiences in the southern region of Africa, close to where we would live, brought excitement and apprehension at the same time. Mzilikazi had been a friend to Moffat.

Most missionaries who came to this part of Africa before 1900 had died, many prematurely, but not before making valuable contributions. They set up schools, studied various languages and put them into written form with an alphabet, and translated and published religious and educational books.

But not only did the missionaries come, other Europeans came. Cecil Rhodes and his British South Africa Company managed to get Lobengula to sign an agreement, and Europeans arrived in droves. With so many coming, the Shona religious leaders advised the Matabele to revolt. This war brought the deaths of many whites and Africans but ultimately the death of Lobengula and the defeat of the Matabele. The Mashona rebellion was also squashed. The Portuguese moved eastward. In 1897, the British South Africa Company was the recognized governing body until 1923 when Southern Rhodesia became a colony of Great Britain. Africans had been relocated, tribes had been split up, and the average African did not trust a white-skinned European. That was the political situation we would enter.

But we would not be alone, because others were feeling God's pull to this place where people needed Jesus. Not only were the Dotsons and Bowlins already serving there with the FMB, two single missionaries, nurse Monda Marlar and teacher Mary Brooner, would arrive in Southern Rhodesia just after we were to be appointed as missionaries in October 1952. We and David and Susie Lockard, also going to Southern Rhodesia, would be appointed in a special service at the same place God whispered in my ear that I would be a medical missionary—Ridgecrest. We also got word that Gene and Dot Kratz would be joining the team. It was a relief to know that Giles and I and our little son would face our new careers with other fellow missionaries. And we heard that there were a few African believers who were blazing the trail with the Bowlins and Dotsons, men such as Mr. Sithole, Mr. Ndebele, Rev. Nyathi, Rev. Ngoma, Rev. Moyana, and a Nigerian and his wife, Rev. and Mrs. Ayorinde.

All the details, information, papers to be filled out, and lists could have gotten the best of me. Honestly, I was depending on God just as much as I ever had. I was ready for the move as appearances go. At least I had gotten rid of things I didn't need and bought items that we did need.

But I didn't count on it being so hard to say good-bye, the first of a lifetime of good-byes.

CHAPTER 4

SS *Stella Lykes*

MEME HAD THE house decorated for Christmas as 1952 was coming to a close. The atmosphere of the place seemed considerably thick since no one wanted to mention our departure for missionary service. Gilesie was content playing with his aunts, who were all long-faced when not with the baby. We were taking their only nephew to the "wilds of Africa." My youngest sister was still a young teenager, being 15 years my junior. It seemed as though I couldn't breathe sometimes as I thought about what we were doing to my family.

Staying in my old room with my husband and son, I contemplated my surroundings. This was the room where I had read books that opened my mind to adventures all over the world. Now, I was about to go on my own quest to fulfill God's will with my new family. It was a lot to take in.

We had been busy buying clothing, personal and medical supplies, and food items as well as packing the furniture we would put into crates. But now, reality was setting in that we were indeed moving halfway around the world.

The day came when it was time to say good-bye to my parents and sisters. As we drove out of the yard, MeMe waved slowly from the porch, but Dad walked to the gate and stood. I can still see him—hat tipped just so over his eyes, head turned to one side, arm resting on the fence. I turned around in my seat and strained to see him until I could no longer. Gilesie laughed with joy at riding in the car, patting my cheeks with his chubby hands, blithely unaware of what good-bye meant or the ache in his grandparents' hearts as we headed toward New Orleans to get on the freighter that would take us to Africa.

Despite the difficulty of saying good-bye, we didn't waver on God's call. Monda Marlar, the nurse appointed to Sanyati, had written to let me know that she had just gotten there and already had to deliver a baby on her own. She wrote, "Please hurry!"

Some friends, the Stinebaughs and Alice Caldwell, drove us to New Orleans and the dock. We were going to meet several people in New Orleans. Giles's mother, Ami, planned to help us with Gilesie for the few days before we left. The Lockards and Kratzes would be on the ship too. There were a couple of hiccups with exporting the truck that would be our transportation once we docked in Cape Town, South Africa. This heavy-duty, four-wheel-drive Dodge truck had been designed to drive in the North African campaign during the war. We named it the Powerful 20 because 20 couples had pooled the funds that bought it for us. It had been sent to the dock. Fortunately, our ship's captain delayed the departure for some reason or other, and we were able to get our goods processed correctly and in time. We actually were able to move from our cheap motel to our cabin on the ship on January 31, 1953, although we didn't leave port until four days later. Ami even slept with us in our tiny cabin that had three pullout berths for sleeping. Gilesie slept in his playpen that we set up on the floor. The ship had two cabins on each side. We three missionary couples had three, and a young, male member of the Lykes family occupied the fourth.

The freighter, the SS *Stella Lykes*, was not a cruise line for wealthy passengers. It was owned by the Lykes Brothers Steamship Company of New Orleans, and this particular ship was named after the wife of the cofounder and vice-president of the company. It was not the original SS *Stella Lykes*. The first ship by this name was actually sunk by a German U-boat when it was torpedoed in April 1942 off the coast of Africa. The second ship by that name also was torpedoed by the Germans. Thankfully World War II was over so that there was no chance for our *Stella* to be sunk!

February 3 came, and the captain finally announced we would be leaving that day. Ami gave the three of us hugs, tears flowing, when it was time to say good-bye, promising her intercessory prayers for us each day. It was an emotional moment, and it signified for us a new course in life—one that would be filled with good-byes, new adventures, and challenges. Fog on the Mississippi River kept us from leaving at 7:00 A.M., but we eventually pulled anchor after breakfast. Sailing down the river was pleasant and smooth as we slowly headed toward the mouth of the Mississippi, eventually passing the lighthouse. This wasn't too bad! No one was sea sick yet.

But the next day, everyone in our party got out the Dramamine to diminish the nausea. Giles, being a sailor, was not seasick; thankfully, neither was Gilesie nor I. David Lockhard and Dot Kratz couldn't keep anything down. The pleasant ride of the first day turned into a nightmare the second, and we had only just passed Miami! Susie Lockhard came down with the flu and had a fever of over 102 degrees. I'm sure the crew wondered whether or not some of us would have the fortitude to survive a boat ride, must less to live in Africa! Gene wasn't affected and ended up taking care of his wife and little seasick daughter.

The fresh air became my greatest ally to not getting nauseated. Even in the chill of the wind, I figured if I could look at the sea, breathe deeply, and sit in a chair with a blanket, I could survive. The weather for the most part was beautiful—the sky bright blue, the sea deep blue, the cool breeze constantly blowing. When we were not on deck, Gilesie wanted to be with the crew. He and Becca Kratz, who was about two years old, were the only children on board, so they provided entertainment for everyone. Captain King became fast friends with him and held him while Gilesie played with the pencil sharpener on his desk. Mr. King looked like the typical captain—fairly tall, clean cut, quiet, and polite. I did notice that he had a tattoo on his left forearm that must have been created to cover a deep scar. It made me wonder. The radio operator, Sparks, was Gilesie's favorite. He was short, balding, and jovial, with a deep New Yorker accent. At ten months old, our little scamp would sit in Sparks's lap at the radio table and try to turn every knob on the board, much to Sparks's amusement.

Even rougher seas came when we were halfway to Cape Town. We kept joking, "Would the captain please stop rocking the boat?!" The only way to get my mind off of it at night was to challenge the men at dominoes. I think I surprised three of the men when I beat them the first time playing.

On Sundays, the three missionary couples, two children, the one other passenger, and some of the crew would participate in a worship service. Giles and the other two missionaries took turns preaching. After we had been traveling ten days, we crossed the equator out in the middle of the Atlantic. As was a custom of the crew, they had an initiation ceremony for those of us who had never crossed the equator at sea (Giles had while serving his country and in fact was proud to be a "golden shellback," since he had crossed the equator at the international date line). The crew dressed up in costumes for the "Royal court of King Neptune." The king was quite the figure draped in his royal robe, which happened to be a sheet, rope wig, and beard, raincoat and hat. His aid was dressed in torn trousers and bandana, minus a few front teeth. Court was then in session. It was a hilarious presentation, and we were presented with "shellback" certificates at the end. We would miss this motley crew once we landed!

After three weeks, I was finally getting my sea legs. Our last day at sea was February 24. We had enjoyed the extra sleep, the leisurely days, and the warm fellowship with new colleagues. On the ship's radio, we began to pick up South African radio stations, hearing advertisements for Camay soap, Schick razor blades, and Shell Oil. With those familiar names, we almost felt like Africa wouldn't be a strange land after all! That night, we began to smell what the sailors called "land." For me, I always associated fishy smells with the ocean, but I stood corrected. The fish odor was smelled only when we got near land. Looking over the railing that dark night, we felt excited and apprehensive. The moonlight reflected off the still water, leaving a shimmering glow on the surface. High above, thousands of brilliant stars twinkled, and the Southern Cross constellation reminded us of the God we served. In our final prayer service on the voyage, we and our now close friends sang "Blest Be the Tie" and read the Twenty-third Psalm. It was our last night to be rocked to sleep.

In all the excitement of the next morning, we were awakened by the captain to see the view at 4:45 A.M. It was right before dawn. We hurried to the ship's bridge and saw what seemed to be a fairyland. The city of Cape Town was spread out before us in the shadows of the magnificent Table Mountain and the Lion's Head and Rump. Around the edge of the bay, a myriad of lights glittered, reaching partway up the sides of the mountains. It was breathtaking! The ship waited in Table Bay until dawn when a tug boat came to greet us. The captain of that boat looked like a king dressed in his uniform. The tug pulled the ship to the dock by 7:30 A.M. Gilesie seemed to sense the excitement as we could see men on bicycles, double-decker buses and streetcars, and road signs in Afrikaans, the daughter language of Dutch spoken in South Africa. After we ate a hurried breakfast on the ship, the customs officials swarmed the deck, and we began filling out declaration forms. We had some problems importing our guns and baby food jars but with great effort and tipping, our items cleared.

The cars and crates were unloaded by a huge crane, and our hearts sank when the crane fell on one of our crates. I had visions of broken china. Susie was nearly in tears about it! But it ended up being our medical supplies, and nothing was damaged except an operating table that received a tiny dent. We said our farewells and disembarked, stepping onto African soil for the first time.

The obvious modern society in South Africa would be a strong contrast for our final destination. In Cape Town, we purchased more supplies that we had been instructed to buy: a waterproof, tropical pith helmet and kerosene refrigerator and iron. These items were crated and put on the large truck with our crates brought from the States. We set out with the other couples in our vehicles filled to the gills with things we'd need for the next few weeks. As our caravan of vehicles got closer to Southern Rhodesia after a few days of driving slowly through South Africa, we appreciated the beauty of Africa.

There were steep, winding roads through densely wooded forests along the coast. Turning north at Port Elizabeth, we traveled toward Bloemfontein. Once when we got lost, we saw several villages of huts. In the late evening sunlight, the huts looked like hundreds of beehives against the mountainsides. Gathered around the huts were women cooking over open fires in big pots while others ground corn using a small stone against a large one. The men lounged on the grass. The children were playing like children anywhere in the world. Before reaching an inn one night, we saw three ridges in the distance, the Hogsback. The way the individual ridges spread out together really did look like an old razorback.

Johannesburg was a large city. At the place where we stopped for a meal, we met Uncle Charlie. He owned the establishment. He was a burly Dutch-looking man, a big game hunter. In his restaurant were many trophies of hunting successes. Uncle Charlie had personally killed about 80 or so lions on his farm. I had never met a "great white hunter" like this man. In Johannesburg, we were able to visit the hospital at the University of Witwatersrand. There were many interesting cases such as a baby who was ten days post-op for a tracheoesophageal fistula, an abnormal connection between the esophagus and the trachea that causes breathing problems if not remedied surgically. Another child was terminal with intestinal atresia, the closure of the intestine. A severely malnourished one-year-old was recovering from shigellosis, an acute bacterial infection of the lining of the intestines.

Most of these cases were things I had only read about in textbooks. I wasn't even in remote Sanyati yet.

We easily got through the border post out of South Africa, but it took hours to get through the Rhodesian border post at the Limpopo River with our items, especially the guns. On our way finally, the roads in Southern Rhodesia hinted that we had crossed into a different country. It was hard to believe we were there. I had to pinch myself. Years had passed by since God told me that I would be a medical missionary. An indescribable feeling of gratitude to my Lord encompassed me, and I felt blessed. He had gotten me this far, and there was no doubt that He could see Giles and me through this journey. Our bodies were tired, but our hearts were full.

We stayed in Bulawayo, a city with streets wide enough for a team of 16 oxen to turn around. Since the Lockhards would be living in this city, we drove by their house. That perked Susie up after the long trip. David was the guest preacher the next afternoon at an African church. It was quite the experience to hear the people sing in their native tongue. After the service, one man asked us how black-skinned people were treated in the States. Racial separation in the States was common, but I felt completely welcomed by the men and women in the gathering. I felt convicted even though I had tried to never show prejudice, unlike the government in Southern Rhodesia. But I had to look in my heart to see if there were any wicked way in me. The Africans in Southern Rhodesia were treated even worse than those in the States who were persecuted because of their skin color. I was determined to show the love of Jesus to all people and be accepted as one who did.

CHAPTER 5

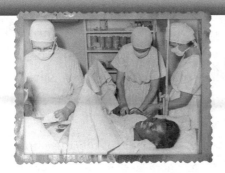

The Sanyati Mission Station

I ENTERED INTO a world unfamiliar and daunting. It began on The Road to Sanyati from Gatooma. We called it The Road because basically, there was no other road I knew of that compared in respect to condition.

The first 16 miles was a strip road, and I guess it wasn't too bad if judged against a road in an impoverished rural region of the United States. We went about 35 miles per hour on this first section. The second section was gravel and wasn't unbearable for a few miles, but it got worse and worse. Several bad dips existed, filled with soft foul-smelling mud, water, tall grass, and sharp stones. Short poles often were laid across rather large potholes. Then there were the tree stumps. Trying to anticipate and dodge the stumps in The Road was more challenging than I can describe. The last section of The Road was a nightmare. It ran through elephant country, and Ralph Bowlin had said that he had come upon a herd not too long ago. Ralph also mentioned that lions, leopards, hyenas, and wild dogs were known to inhabit the area as well. To say The Road resembled a road at this point is an exaggeration. I asked Ralph why there were charred remains of fires along the sides. Without hesitation, he said they were from the fires made by people whose cars had gotten stuck overnight or even longer. Once, he had ridden a bicycle from Sanyati to Gatooma because The Road was worse than what I was experiencing on my first trip!

Because we had departed in the middle of the afternoon, it was dark by the time we got to the most terrible part. There is no darkness like the night in rural Africa when there is no moon. The lights of the car seemed pitifully ineffective as we looked out into the bush. My imagination ran wild concerning what might be lurking just a few feet away from the car, and I could envision myself holding little Gilesie as I hunkered down by a fire on the roadside. It was a scary thought! At last, we made it, much to my relief. Betty had supper waiting when we pulled into the station at 9:00 P.M. Since everything was pitch black, I could not see the station as we arrived. We were exhausted. The Bowlins insisted we take their bed right after we ate.

Early the next morning, however, was glorious. Varieties of birds I had never seen were chirping by 5:00 A.M. as the sun rose, and I was anxious to see the work that had started on the hospital building. The two-room mud and pole hut had become the dispensary and would serve as a temporary clinic. Monda had been treating people's ailments with the little medicine that she had. I was impressed that the Bowlins were already conversing well in Shona. I had to admire this couple. Not only were they running things at the station and overseeing the hospital construction, but they had given up a bedroom to our family and another one to Monda and Mary until our houses could be built. With all of us in the house together, it was quite small, but we managed OK. Each night, we enjoyed devotions together before going to bed at 9:30. The generator was always turned off at 10:00 P.M., and the lights were dim anyway after dark.

Soon after we moved to Sanyati, Gilesie celebrated his first birthday. It was made special when an African man, Daniel, told me that there were some girls from the school who wanted to see me. Outside were five shy girls. They each gave me a penny from their own earnings to give to Gilesie. I was truly touched. It was a lovely thing for them to do since they had very little money.

I visited my first hut on a medical call shortly after his birthday. It was square, made of mud and poles, with the only light coming in from the cracks in the walls. A premature baby boy had been born two months too early to the wife of a young male teacher, Abel Nziramasanga, and it was lying on a cot of towels with another towel covering it. He was very small, about three pounds, and would not nurse. I wasn't sure what to do, so I brought the mother and the baby back to the station. Giles emptied out a wooden box that he had made for our typewriter during the trip and turned it into a bed for the baby. We used two hot water bottles and a blanket to create a makeshift incubator and dressed the baby in a little flannelette garment that had belonged to Gilesie. I taught the mother how to use a breast pump, sterilized some of the milk in the empty baby food jars that I had saved, and then fed the infant with a dropper. On his first go, he drank the milk well—about half an ounce. The mother and baby stayed at our makeshift clinic, and I fed him every three or four hours, getting up during the night. That was his only chance. I think the people were surprised that I took such an interest in this little baby, but he was my first patient. We didn't have our own house, we couldn't unpack our belongings, the hospital wasn't finished, so I focused on the survival of this child.

The first night I hardly slept; I was afraid the child might die and people would think it was my fault. That's not how I wanted my career in Africa to start. So I prayed and prayed that God would keep this child alive. The next morning, in my sleepy state, I went outside and came upon a banded cobra in the yard. So worried for Gilesie, I found something to kill it. That night I lay in bed seeing that cobra in my mind. Between feeding the African baby and imagining Gilesie being bitten by a snake, I didn't get much sleep that night either. I kept feeding the newborn by dropper for two weeks or so until he was able to suck. It was a day of celebration when the infant began to nurse! The teacher named his son Ralph, and I prayed that God would use this tiny one to one day serve the Lord. God had saved him for a purpose, and I was grateful God answered my prayers.

I began to hear people calling me *Mai Chiremba*. With my limited language skills, I had to ask what it meant. Translated literally, it was "Mother (or Mrs.) Doctor." I was happy with my new name. It didn't take me long to find out how important names were, because in Shona culture a name characterized a person. It was a good thing to have a respectable name.

Even without a hospital completed, other patients heard that two doctors were at Sanyati. By the flickering light of a kerosene lamp, I began an intravenous drip on a baby girl with severe burns on 30 percent of her body. Because we did not have our equipment yet, Giles and I rigged up the one bottle of IV fluids we had on a stand made from a broom handle on top of a cabinet. We kept fluids going by stomach tube, warming the solution on a little Coleman burner. We were able to stabilize her before taking her to the hospital in Gatooma for skin grafts.

We had cases of encephalitis and learned about falciparum malaria before we had a lab to confirm a diagnosis. The little son of our nursing orderly was severely ill with dysentery. Fortunately, I had medicine brought along for our son if he became ill and made the decision to give her son this treatment. As the child's mother and I knelt on the floor of that old clinic building, sponging his convulsing body to lower the temperature, praying together, our tears flowed. God's presence was felt; He cemented a love between us that lasted. Her son responded to the medicine and lived. Later she would become the first African director of the nursing service at the hospital.

The first time our son became ill, I feared the worst. He had a high fever and before I even examined him, I was afraid he might have malaria. I even cried to Giles, believe it or not, "God sent us out to this wilderness with our baby boy, and we don't even have a doctor to take him to!" When I pulled myself together, it wasn't hard for Giles and me to determine that our son had a throat infection. We treated him with antibiotics, and he was fine in no time. It was amazing how my mind could imagine the most horrible thing that could happen when it concerned my own family!

Giles had difficult obstetric deliveries, often performed with inadequate instruments by lantern light. A woman named Joyce was one of these patients. Her unborn baby had been dead some time before she arrived at the clinic. She had a severe infection. Giles performed surgery, and then she was treated with medicine to clear up the infection. She was slow to respond. As we sought to share the gospel with her, she turned her face to the wall and put the pillow over her head. But finally she listened and gave her life to Christ before we transferred her to the tuberculosis hospital in Gatooma. Some months later, she returned home from the hospital and was baptized. Her radiant joy in the Lord was a powerful witness to her family and those in her village. Later we heard that she had been out in the fields helping to plant corn. It was a hot day, and she suddenly collapsed and died with a pulmonary hemorrhage.

Our first year in Southern Rhodesia, 1953, was a historic time as well. The Federation of Central Africa (Zimbabwe and Zambia) and Nyasaland (Malawi) was formed as a British state in which Southern Rhodesia was a self-governing colony, and Northern Rhodesia (Zambia) and Nyasaland were protectorates. The figurehead of this colony would be a young woman, who went up a tree as a princess (staying in a luxury tree house while on her honeymoon in Kenya) and came down a queen the next day due to the death of her father, King George VI. Queen Elizabeth II's coronation was in June 1953 and with the queen mother, she came to Bulawayo for the Rhodes Centenary on July 3, which most of our missionaries attended. I happened to have a medical concern that needed attention in Bulawayo while there, so I missed the festivities that celebrated the 100th anniversary of Cecil Rhodes's birth. The Kratzes, however, were presented to the young queen, which was quite a talked-about moment within our mission.

With the knowledge that I lived in a British colony, it really didn't change the fact that I was acutely aware that I lived in Africa. Many distinctive and things new to me were apparent: The weird baobab tree with its tuft of branches topping a thick, stout trunk and its fruit, the hard oval pod filled with cream of tartar, which the Africans like to munch . . . the graceful slender arms of the candelabra tree, which curved upward to the tropical sky . . . the glory of the Southern Cross in the clear heavens, and the eerie laugh of the hyena and the beat of African drums near our house at night . . . the broken piece of rock embedded deep into a tire . . . the rows of huts with inevitable goats, chickens, and skinny dogs running about . . . the little hut in the cornfield where the son guarded in order to frighten the baboons that delighted in walking down a row, plucking an ear, dropping the one just picked, and walking on down the row, plucking an ear, and so on, leaving a trail of green ears until he reached the end of the row and stopped to eat the last ear . . . the homemade beer made in the big, black cauldrons, which created patients needing stitches by Monday . . . scars on bodies made intentionally for beauty where medicine had been applied by the witch doctor. The people pulled on our heartstrings as we began to see the fear and superstition, extreme poverty, and the lost condition of a people without Jesus Christ. Our first year was one of constant cultural learning without taking a course to prepare. We were thrust into the situation head first with experience as our teacher.

Not many months after the hospital was opened, I was called to go to a village for a woman who was unable to have her baby. Arriving there, I found that she had been in labor over a day with the old *ambuyas* trying to pull a premature, breech baby out of her. I managed to deliver a baby boy, already dead. Then I discovered that there was a twin, but it was also dead upon delivery. We took the young woman back to the hospital for a blood transfusion and antibiotic therapy.

When she was ready to go home, her mother came to us. With tears, she said, "Two years ago no doctor was here and no hospital was here. My older daughter had this same trouble having her baby, and Missionary Bowlin tried to take her to town. It was during the rains, and the truck broke down. She and her baby died by the roadside. The missionaries prayed for doctors. If the doctors and the hospital were not here now, this second daughter of mine would be dead too. Her life was saved because of the doctor God sent. How we thank God for sending people to help us! We want to serve that God."

Stunned by her words, I realized the story of her first daughter was the story God used to lead us to Southern Rhodesia. This family's story had come full circle in their lives and ours. My heart toward the Lord was full and running over. We were here because God brought us to save the life of this young woman and countless others in the name of Jesus.

Hearing stories like this brought awe. But we faced many challenges! I guess our biggest adjustment was to the primitive way we had to doctor. When we unpacked our crates for the hospital, the people couldn't believe the supplies and equipment were for the Sanyati Baptist Hospital. We couldn't use everything when we first started, because the construction of the hospital was going slowly. We experienced some time without the use of the generator, so a few young boys and I had to haul water in large drums loaded on the back of the truck. The clinic we worked out of had a concrete floor and low asbestos roof. With only two small rooms, we used one for examining patients, the other for inpatients. In another temporary building, there were two tiny rooms for patients, one cot to each room. It was not easy to treat patients during the severe influenza epidemic in those first few months. We put people in storerooms on cots we had unpacked from our crates. Most of the severely ill patients and all the surgical cases still had to be taken to Gatooma. Often the people refused to go to the government hospital, and we had to care for them the best we could. It wasn't easy. And in the midst of this momentous year, I found out I was pregnant!

Over and over, I was reminded that God loved me. If I didn't believe it, I may have gone home to the States. We somehow made it through that first year, and our house was finally finished enough to move in after living with the Bowlins for many months. The Kratzes moved to Sanyati after the Dotsons returned from the States, so our little station was growing in personnel. Dot was an experienced lab technician. As the end of this first year was coming to a close, I was relieved when Christmas Day 1953 came. That's when we officially dedicated the building of the new, small Baptist hospital. We were committed to being God's hands of mercy and healing to souls and bodies.

But we would face a spiritual battle—one that we didn't expect.

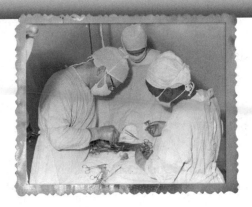

The Insidious Worm

IT WAS A sunny day, and I finally had time to do laundry. David had been born in April of 1954, two days before Gilesie's second birthday, and cloth diapers were overwhelming due to only having a gasoline-powered, wringer washing machine. It was a nasty chore but had to be done. With no electric power, the noise of generators and machines fueled with petrol became as common as the noises of the bush at night. I was content knowing that our second born was healthy. Giles delivered him at our new hospital, the first FMB missionary kid to be born in Rhodesia and the Sanyati Baptist Hospital. We were both grateful that there were no complications during the delivery. Gilesie seemed quite fascinated with his new baby brother.

Fortunately, I hired someone to help me with some of the housekeeping and child-care tasks, or I would have never had time to be a doctor as well as mother and wife. The kerosene-powered refrigerator had to be defrosted often, which left me in a sour mood every time. I had to refill the tank to keep the refrigerator working. Gratefully, I was adept at cooking on a wood stove. I made all the clothes for our sons on my treadle sewing machine. All the clothes and diapers washed had to be hung out to dry, but I couldn't fold and put away the clothes until everything, even our underwear, was pressed by our kerosene-heated iron. The reason for this extra measure was that unfortunately, Sanyati was in the zone for *putzi* flies. Those pesky insects would lay their eggs on wet clothing hung outside. When a line-dried garment was worn, if not ironed, the eggs would hatch, and the larvae would burrow into the skin of the wearer, causing a boil that stayed sore until the worm was forced to pop out. Quite disgusting! With a toddler and baby and our dirty medical uniforms, we had a lot of laundry. I did not even want to think about one of those worms growing beneath the skin of my little ones.

The bothersome maggot in a boil, however, was not nearly as bothersome as the way Satan tried to worm his way into our medical ministry. Every time we turned around, we discovered superstition and witchcraft, often creating a barrier for helping those in need and sharing the gospel.

Early one morning, a man came seeking a doctor because his niece was stiff and could not talk. Giles went in the truck to the *kraal* (huts of a family clan) and found the child, who had the symptoms of tubercular meningitis. He brought the child back to the hospital and although we could not confirm the diagnosis, we were sure that was what she had. Because we had no way to properly treat her yet, we encouraged the family to let us take her to the Gatooma hospital. The father was in another village working and since he made all the family decisions, the mother refused to move her daughter without his consent. The uncle went for him and upon finding the father and explaining the situation, the father was furious that the mother had allowed Giles to take the daughter to our hospital in the first place. He steadfastly declined to have her taken to town but did allow her to stay with us three days. If no improvement in three days, he would personally collect her to take her back to the *kraal*.

Three days was surely not enough time for a child that sick to recover, especially when we didn't have the proper facility or medicine with which to treat her. As the pediatrician, I was really upset that a father would basically put a death sentence on his daughter's head. Sure enough, three days later, the father showed up at the hospital one night and demanded that we transport his daughter back to their home place. Later that evening, she was put on a stretcher and carried in the bed of the truck back to the *kraal*. As we parked by the hut, people began to come from nowhere to watch. When we prayed before leaving, there were 30 or more people standing around. It was so needless for this child to die, but I knew she would.

Because the small village was not far from the mission station, we heard loud wailing in the wee hours of the morning coming from that direction. We knew that the witch doctor probably had been summoned. Before dawn, we heard more wailing and surmised that the child had passed. It did not have to happen. Over and over it was demonstrated to us that Christ is the only answer to the needs of this world.

With our limited understanding of the African culture and beliefs before arriving, Giles and I faced a spiritual realm that we had never experienced before. I'm not sure if we could have been properly prepared for the fear and superstition of the people and the powerful influences of Satan through the witch doctors and revered *midzimu* (ancestral spirits). It became normal for us to see patients with cuts made by a witch doctor on their bodies to let out the spirits causing disease or sickness. One man told us the witch doctor said it would take powerful medicine to cure him since he had already taken the white man's medicine. People were told by witch doctors that the white man's medicine would make sickness or disease "walk through their bodies."

The Rhodesian government had the power to arrest and imprison practicing witch doctors but because practicing witchcraft was kept secret, it was very difficult to make an arrest. It was my opinion that the witch doctor was responsible for many deaths. The witch doctor threw bones, usually sticks with carvings on them, to determine answers for paying customers. We learned a lot over the years about the African's attitude about disease and sickness from Dr. O. M. Munyaradizi, a surgeon in Bulawayo. He said that the people in our area believed that disease was caused by ancestral spirits or by witchcraft. The belief that ancestral spirits made their displeasure known by making the offending relative or family member sick was widespread. Witchcraft was different in that a person could buy poisonous substances made by a witch doctor to either give to a person or use in a ritual against a person. We often saw markings made on people or charms made to ward off spirits; we often saw families consult one another in hushed whispers about what the witch doctor had said. It was frustrating to actually have fear as our main competitor. It made me desire more than anything that our people group would find that Jesus was more powerful than any witch doctor or spirit.

One evening, a man came to our door about the time we were sitting down for our traditional Sunday supper of waffles. Six hours earlier, his wife had been bitten by a deadly black mamba. Why would anyone wait even one minute before running for a doctor? They only lived five kilometers away! Of course, when Giles drove the man back to his hut, the woman had been dead for hours. What superstition or fear prevented him from seeking help sooner, for surely he knew she was dead before he came for us!

We had a hopeless cancer patient brought to us whom we advised to go to town for possible x-ray therapy (that was all that was available in the 1950s). They refused and took her home to make the rounds of the witch doctors. When it became obvious to them that the witch doctors couldn't help, they brought her back to us in an advanced stage of the malignancy. Knowing that the greatest thing we could give her was the story of the Lord Jesus, we kept her for a few days so that we could talk with her and relieve some of her suffering. One Sunday while Giles and she conversed, she said that she wanted to become a Christian. How it encouraged us to see her make this decision! When her family insisted on taking her home to die, we were grateful our work had not been in vain, even though we could not heal her body.

A young wife was brought to us from the Gokwe Reserve, many miles away and across the river. She had been sick for months, and her swollen body was covered with hundreds of tiny scars in which a witch doctor had scratched to "let out the poison." The infection from the scratches had actually caused her swelling.

Another young woman was brought to us with swollen legs. After she had been in the hospital a few days, she said her trouble was caused by stepping on a witch doctor's *muti* (potions or charms). She had not seen it on the path until it was too late. It troubled us because she was convinced in her mind that she would never get well. No positive reinforcement came from her family, because they also believed she couldn't get well. Gradually with treatment from us, she was able to sit in a wheelchair or stand. But one night, more family members visited and told her that the white doctors couldn't help her. The next day, she was worse. Again she lay in bed without speaking. We worked with her again, and she improved. Then other relatives convinced her that she had been "witched" and for the third time, her health declined. One morning, she pointed to the bed sheets with terror. Our sheets weren't white due to repeated washing in the iron-rich borehole water; they had taken on a rust color. Because of this, the woman believed that every night the poison came out of her body and stained the sheets red. And it didn't help that all our hospital blankets were red to begin with! Showing her that all the other sheets and blankets in the small ward were also red had no effect. A few days later, relatives slipped in the ward after midnight and took her away, most likely to a witch doctor.

People were afraid of sickness, especially when an illness lasted longer than a week or so. Our house helper named Sunday was losing weight and not feeling well. After examining him, my husband sent him to town for a chest x-ray, because we didn't have all the parts for our machine yet. The doctors found a tumor and wanted him to go to the hospital in Salisbury. But Sunday refused to go. He claimed that there was "something" that started on his right shoulder and "walked" down the right side of his chest, then across to the left side and up the left shoulder. He said the European doctors could not help this. So he was going to the African "doctors" to obtain some powerful medicine that would get rid of this "something."

Giving a blood transfusion or having donors for transfusions was another situation affected by superstition. It was very difficult to get the locals to donate or receive blood since they believed giving or receiving would surely kill a person. They equated blood with life itself. Our first recipient of blood was a woman who had been bleeding two and a half days before someone brought her to us. She was in severe shock. Much to our distress, she was type B, a difficult blood type to match. We finally convinced her husband to allow us to find donors for blood, including him. We tested six people who came for typing and amazingly, two men were B and were able to serve as donors, one being the husband. The next day when she was much better, her husband's gratitude to God and us was inspiring. In fact, when people saw what happened, they said, "She was as dead. She could not sit up or walk. Now she is brought to life again. This is a wonderful thing we have seen!" We felt that the Lord was looking after this woman, and honestly, He was looking out for us as well. Word spread, and school students and station workers were more willing to donate blood. From this point, we were able to demonstrate that the power of human blood to save lives was just a picture of the power of the blood of Jesus to save the sin-sick soul of man.

Four-month-old Peggy was brought to the hospital after a month's illness. The witch doctors had been treating her. She weighed just nine pounds; her hemoglobin, which should have been about 11 grams, was less than 5. Our little David was just two weeks old, but I went to the hospital to give Peggy a blood transfusion that night, and again, and again. She had a severe infection, which required intensive treatment; we were once again grateful for the drugs we had brought. Our national nurses and orderly had never before seen the new antibiotics used for Africans; they had thought these were only for white people. After some time, Peggy went home, happy and well. This was one of the good stories. Most of the helpless "bewitched" babies did not live. The joy of a woman seeing her baby "come back to life" was indescribable. So many women lost babies due to infection, diarrhea, pneumonia, or malnourishment. Word got around that the doctors were bringing babies back to life. Always we would say a life is in God's hands; He helps and blesses. God wants to save all people who will come to Him, even more than we wanted to save lives from death.

I'd look at my two sweet babies and feel blessed that they were thriving. One afternoon after the boys' naps, I took Gilesie and little David outside while I took a few minutes to work in the garden. Gilesie was busily helping me dig in the earth and suddenly he looked up at me, smiled, and said, "Nani, Gilesie is happy." He skipped over to where I had laid David on a blanket and entertained his little brother. I smiled and thought of the Bible verse he was currently quoting nonstop in his own version, "The Lord is my Shepherd; I don't want!" Those little boys taught me much about contentment and happiness. They didn't have a care in the world, and my Jesus was totally capable of handling all of my cares and burdens.

There was much to encourage us. Several sets of twins were brought to us regularly for treatment but before we came, twins would have been left to die due to superstition. People began to show up when they first got sick. Expecting women started coming for prenatal care, and a few came for delivery. When I saw my first charm tied around a newborn's neck filled with vile bits and pieces of bones, herbs, and who knows what that the witch doctor prepared, I was appalled. What germs loomed in the little pouch that could bring illness to a newborn! So much about hygiene needed to be taught.

Chapter 6

At least mothers were beginning to see that their newborns had a better chance of survival if delivered at our hospital. Their custom was to deliver in a birthing hut, with old grandmothers as midwives. The woman in labor would squat with the help of the grandmothers so that the baby could be delivered on the dirt floor that had been polished with cow dung. The cord would be cut with a hoe or anything handy. The miracle was that all babies born in this primitive environment didn't die of neonatal tetanus. It broke my heart when new babies were brought in with this diagnosis.

Doing our first operating room procedure under anesthetic to repair a broken femur in a young school boy brought so much excitement on the mission station, one would have thought it was a major operation! Another one of our first operations was on Jane, who worked for the hospital. She was diagnosed with an abdominal tumor. It became infected, and Jane was very ill. We had to remove the tumor. There were many whispers over this event, and I began to wonder what was up with our African staff. I could tell that they did not want to tell me, but I eventually learned that the wife of another one of the hospital workers was apparently a witch and had reportedly caused Jane's illness by a curse. In fact, Jane was extremely disturbed one day after the operation when the witch came to visit her at the hospital. There was so much we needed to learn about the culture.

We were thrilled that Dot Kratz ran our little lab, where we also set up a sterilizer and autoclave. With definite diagnoses of malaria, bilharzias, and infectious diseases, the lab and Dot were answers to prayer. Our hospital was improving, despite the obstacles and spiritual warfare.

I prayed a lot that first year at Sanyati. For the first time, I realized the meaning of Ephesians 6:12 that "we do not wrestle against flesh and blood, but against principalities, against powers, against the rulers of the darkness of this age, against spiritual hosts of wickedness in the heavenly places." Spiritual warfare became a reality for Giles and me. It seemed like countless opportunities arose for the devil to needle us. If it wasn't the frustrating witchcraft pervasive in our area, it was the little things that "got my goose." The Road was a real test of my endurance. Giles or one of us missionaries often would have to go to town to pick up supplies or transport a patient to the Gatooma hospital, many times twice a week. During the rainy season, it took a day to get to town and a day to get back. One time, the power wagon broke down on The Road, and Giles had to walk 25 miles round-trip to get a main spring to repair the vehicle. Finally, we got one of the workers at the hospital to earn a driver's license so someone else could make those trips.

The generators that we needed for electricity became a thorn in the flesh. Repairs were endless, and it would sometimes take months to get one properly repaired. Once we thought we might have lights for a while, something would happen to another generator. Just as the generated electricity wasn't reliable, neither was the water. There were two boreholes: one to supply the general station, the other for the hospital. We had a motor to run each pump but while working on the new wiring, one of the electricians let one of them burn out. So we had to run one motor to the other borehole to keep both tanks filling. Then the support for one of the 2,500-gallon tanks collapsed, and the tank fell to the ground and was crushed useless. The stand had been put up a few weeks before by a plumber, but he did a poor job of it obviously. So we had to resort to using a 500-gallon tank, and the motor had to be carried back and forth even more frequently between the two. With all the various station problems, Giles and I figured it took between two and four hours per day with just those tasks. Ralph Bowlin, Gene Kratz, and Giles were supervising different building projects between the *kraal* schools, hospital, and Sanyati school dormitories. For Giles, this responsibility had to be scheduled in between time spent in treating patients.

Nothing was ever easy or efficient. I knew more than ever that Romans 8:37–39 was true: "Yet in all these things we are more than conquerors through Him who loved us. For I am persuaded that neither death nor life, nor angels nor principalities nor powers, nor things present nor things to come, nor height nor depth, nor any other created thing, shall be able to separate us from the love of God which is in Christ Jesus our Lord." I could have easily added, "The Road, nor generators, nor black mambas, nor *putzi* flies, nor witch doctors" to those verses! Even those things couldn't separate me from God's love and care. I learned to claim the fact that "He who is in you is greater than he who is in the world" (1 John 4:4). And yes, I also could quote from memory: "I have learned in whatever state I am, to be content" (Philippians 4:11). Gilesie's version of the Twenty-third Psalm repeated in my head: "The Lord is my Shepherd; I don't want!" The school of prayer and the Word of God became my education. I would need that education when I faced the enemy head-on more than once.

CHAPTER 7

The Uttermost

NEVER FAR FROM our thoughts was not only to bring the gospel to the Sanyati Reserve but also to find a way to reach the many people in extremely remote places beyond our area. Giles, Ralph, Clyde Dotson, and national pastors discussed the possibility of making trips deep into Gokwe and even faraway places such as Northern Rhodesia and Nyasaland. Our African brothers were very keen to evangelize. The love we shared with our dear friends such as the Nyathis, Sitholes, and later, the Muchecheteres grew into deep friendships. It was a pleasure to be on a team and see their enthusiasm. Their love was the kind of love that I wanted and prayed to have. While the United States and even the colony where we lived had increasing racial tension, we thrived in our developing relationships. In so many ways, these men and women were my teachers, and I had a lot to learn about living a selfless Christian life as our special friends did.

On Sundays since we had arrived, I taught Sunday School to the school girls who boarded at the mission station before Giles left to preach at three or more preaching points. He first attended to critical patients then left, returning about 5:00 P.M. I stayed at Sanyati in case medical emergencies occurred. We always believed that the primary and foremost purpose for medical missions was to use the opportunities to heal as opportunities to share Christ. Mrs. Nyathi, an outstanding Christian woman, believed that the hospital was helping to advance the gospel. I remember her saying, "Everywhere the people say it is the work of the hospital that makes people know that Baptists do good work. When they see how sick people are cared for and how Jesus is preached to them, then they say that Baptists love people and want to help them. This is very important for people to know. It helps many people want to know Jesus." Because of the strife in the country, it especially was important to be a witness of love and concern.

Whereas all our friends in the States thought Sanyati Reserve was the uttermost, according to Acts 1:8, to us Sanyati was our Jerusalem. Our Judea included some of the new preaching points. Our Samaria was the Gokwe Reserve. But our ends of the earth were Northern Rhodesia and especially, Nyasaland.

Gokwe was a vast area, much larger than the Sanyati Reserve. Because it was across the river, and there was no bridge, access to Gokwe was only during the dry season of July through September. Not many months after we arrived, people began walking or riding a bicycle long distances to reach us. They waded across the river during the dry season. Many of these people had never heard the name of Jesus even uttered. But at the hospital, many from Gokwe were healed and heard the gospel. The burden of our hearts was that they went home as little babes in the Lord with no one to teach them, unable to read the Bible, unable to grow in knowledge and understanding of our Lord. We were very happy when the mission had a raft made with steel drums to use to cross the river so that people could come to the hospital during the rainy season. We hired a man to sail the raft back and forth. The news of the hospital and Jesus began to spread. We earnestly prayed that a doctor would come to set up clinics in Gokwe and that more missionaries would answer God's call to come.

One day, parents came from Gokwe bringing their baby girl to the hospital. There were deep third-degree burns on her bottom and thighs and extensive second-degree burns on her legs and abdomen. She was only five months old. They told us the sister had dropped her in the fire, but later one of our nurses heard that both parents had been drunk and were sleeping it off when the baby rolled into the fire. Their other little girl had tried to rouse them in vain, and finally the child managed to pull the baby out of the fire. For a while, we had hopes that little Elizabeth would respond to our intensive treatment, but she became much worse.

Late one evening, Monda, Giles, and I went to the hospital to check on the injured baby since her condition was critical. Fluids were dripping into her vein. She was also on oxygen. The parents sat by the bed, eyes heavy from lack of sleep, faces creased with anxiety. Giles sat down to talk with them. In the adjoining room, Monda and I waited and prayed. Giles explained that their baby was dying but that Elizabeth would be with Jesus. He told them that they too could be with Jesus when they died if they trusted in Him. Very simply, Giles explained the gospel story while the parents listened. Then the father said, "But, doctor, how can I be saved? There have been no schools where I live, and I have not even learned to read. I can't read about these things in the Bible of which you speak. There are no churches in our village, and no preachers have come to explain about Jesus to us. How can I believe?" In the other room, I wondered too how this man and wife could grasp the wonderful truth of the love of Jesus for them, the death of Jesus for their sins, and the salvation that comes from trusting in Jesus. It was a strange story to this family. Thank God, however, that the Holy Spirit worked in their hearts. As the mission station lights went out at 10:00 P.M., and we continued to sit in the lamplight, the Spirit was there. First the mother, then the father quietly said that they wanted to trust in Jesus. As we all prayed together, our hearts were thrilled again at the power that is able "to save to the uttermost those who come to God through Him" (Hebrews 7:25).

The next morning, the life of little Elizabeth slipped quietly away. Our national minister conducted the service for the parents, and she was buried in the swamp land as is their custom for a child under three. Her parents returned home but came back to visit several times. We felt that they had a genuine experience with the Lord. Still there was no church, no preacher, and no one to disciple them as they tried to live Christian lives in their faraway village.

We had heard many things about Gokwe. It was known as a place where powerful witch doctors lived. One patient from there brought his own *muti* from a witch doctor to put in his food and to rub on his body. No wonder he didn't improve during the two weeks under our care! The children from Gokwe were often severely malnourished and vitamin deficient, crippled as a result of polio, or had various other serious illnesses. Many people died in Gokwe because of the lack of proper medical attention. Different tribes lived in this area due to resettlement by the government including the Shangwe, Ndebele, and the very remote tribe, the Tonga.

We had heard about the Tonga. This tribe originally had lived on the Zambezi River but when the government dammed the river for a source of electricity, the Tonga were moved by the truckloads many kilometers away from water. They did not know how to be farmers—they were fishermen. Many people starved, and they resorted to eating the food found in tree bean pods or roots of trees. They had what we considered to be unique practices, such as knocking out their girls' four front teeth, a sign of beauty to them, but it also allowed them to smoke the long, traditional gourd pipes. They believed in a god called Lezu and strongly venerated the spirits.

There became such an intense longing within Giles and me, our fellow missionaries, the pastors such as Rev. Maposa and his wife, the newly established chapter of WMU, and the believers on our hospital staff to see the gospel spread into Gokwe. We needed a seminary to train leaders, and we needed more missionaries to reach Gokwe and other remote places. Already two new couples, John and Marie Cheyne and Gerald and Eunice Harvey, were appointed to missionary service to join us in Southern Rhodesia but not in our uttermost.

In July 1954, Giles, Clyde Dotson, Pastor Nyekanyeka, and Pastor Ngomo took a trip into Nyasaland. The mission had plans to expand into Northern Rhodesia, but the opportunity to make a vision trip into Nyasaland came about first. This protectorate was definitely the end of the earth. David Livingstone had explored this area. He named the land Nyasaland when he heard the people there referring to the massive lake as Nyasa. Livingstone named the largest town Blantyre after his own birthplace in Scotland. While exploring the possibility of eventually establishing a mission there, Giles met up with an Anglican pastor. Unfortunately, this man did not particularly want the Baptists invading his area of work. Giles explained that Baptists didn't want to compete; they simply wanted to join the efforts to evangelize Nyasaland.

At that time, the vast majority of the tribe in the area surrounding Blantyre were of the Muslim faith. My understanding was that Arab slave traders came into the country years before and captured the local people, forcing them to carry ivory to the coast before the Arabs sold them as slaves. Somehow through this contact, the Africans accepted a form of Islam, mixing it with their own traditional beliefs. Our group discovered that most of the Muslims in Nyasaland were third and fourth generation.

Dreams and plans were made on that trip to see the gospel brought to Nyasaland and to neighboring Northern Rhodesia, which was home to the Bemba, Ngoni, Tonga, Lozi, and unknown tribes. Our young mission prayed fervently for doors to open into those places.

Our enemy, Satan, had a different agenda, and we experienced some painful tragedies before our first furlough in 1956. The first thing that happened that threw us all for a loop was that we found a malignant spinal-cord tumor in our friend, Pastor Nyathi. There was nothing we could do for him because the cancer was advanced. Not too many weeks after the diagnosis, he called to his wife, my dear friend, about 4:00 A.M. and asked her to pray with him. She asked him to pray first, but he said that he was too weak. So she did. Then he told her that he would be in heaven by 10:00 A.M. that morning. And sure enough, he was.

It really shook Giles up when he went to their home the morning of Pastor Nyathi's death. He and Gene gently took the body of their friend and placed it in the back of Gene's car to be driven back to the hospital and prepared for burial. Just as they were putting the body in the car, the sky rapidly became so dark and dusty that they could not see. A whirlwind suddenly blew up, tearing about half of the asbestos roofing sheets off the school building where the car was parked. We always wondered if that were God's way of acknowledging the passing of such a godly man. We remembered that Elijah had been taken up in a whirlwind.

During the funeral, Mrs. Nyathi was completely calm, unlike most of the women who wailed during funerals. She had her five children around her, aged 2 through 14. Giles, Gene, and Pastor Sithole all spoke. Pastor Sithole preached from the 30th chapter of Job about God lifting the spirit of man in the wind. The nationals were just as affected by the episode of the whirlwind as we were. Giles had lost a friend that day. I didn't know how my friend could possibly survive without her husband. We sang a chorus together that Mrs. Nyathi and her children used to sing to her husband. I don't think I've ever been moved as much by anything. He was a man who was one of the first Baptist leaders, who had been trained at the seminary in South Africa, and now he was dead.

After the funeral, Giles and I packed the car so that our family could go on a vacation. We just needed to get away. We drove to Victoria Falls. Seeing the magnificent waterfalls for the first time, we were awed by the majesty of God. We took a boat tour for tourists and rode up the Zambezi River, winding around several islands before we docked on Monkey Island. It didn't take us long to understand why it was called by this name. I had never seen so many monkeys in my life! Gilesie had a bag of cookies, and the monkeys flocked around him as he threw pieces to them. Back in the boat, we saw several hippos. We spent a night in a hut at a camp. Before coming home, we stayed at Wankie (Hwange) Game Reserve where we saw herds of kudu with their twisting spiral horns, bush buck, eland, sable, wart hog, giraffe, a leopard, zebra, ostrich, and of course, elephant. We cooked our own food on a portable cook stove while staying at a rest hut.

That trip gave us time to settle ourselves after the death of our friend. We didn't understand why God allowed this great man to die, but who were we to question God? I looked at Gilesie and little David and wondered how I could possibly raise those boys without my husband. They brought so much joy to our lives. Gilesie made me laugh because he had learned my first name and had actually called me Wana Ann. He looked at me with those big, brown eyes to see what I'd say, so I amused him by saying, "Gilesie, have you learned your Nani's first name?" He'd giggle and say, "Ess." David was amused too, as only a baby can be. He'd look at us with a big grin and a lot of twinkle in his blue eyes. He could get our attention when he wanted something by increasing his volume. David got much joy from tearing up a book and chewing it. Amidst this joy, I couldn't help but think of the Nyathi's five children, now fatherless.

Then we were slammed again. Five months later, when Giles was in Gatooma, Monda and Mary ran to the house to get me at 3:30 A.M. Mrs. Sithole was in labor at seven months. The Sitholes lived at the mission station since her husband was not only a pastor but also our station foreman. I was very concerned and ran up the dark path to the hospital with Monda. Mrs. Sithole had been rushed to Gatooma about a year ago where she had a C-section due to placenta previa. She lost that baby. We had planned to do a C-section on her for this pregnancy at the end of the eighth month so that she would not go into labor and risk rupturing the uterus.

One look when I saw her on the bed at the hospital confirmed my worries. She was in shock and had severe abdominal pain. Her uterus had ruptured. I ran home to get morphine and supplies after I sent someone to get Dot. I left Pastor Sithole standing there panicked. Mary sent for a school girl to sleep at the house with my children so that she could be with us at the hospital and pray. Because our autoclave was out of commission, I retrieved our Coleman stove and pressure cooker to sterilize instruments for surgery. I kept thinking, *Of all nights for Giles to be out of town!* He was the obstetrical surgeon, not I. I knew that Mrs. Sithole's situation was serious and prayed as hard as I could that the Lord would help her live.

Dot got blood from donors for Mrs. Sithole. She had some trouble with the equipment and had to sterilize again. It seemed like nothing was going right. About 7:30 A.M., Mrs. Sithole's blood pressure stabilized, and she seemed to be doing better. I was most worried about the fact that we did not have an anesthetist. I had little experience in anesthesia. Giles was the one who did. But I had no choice. I had to operate. I put her to sleep with drop ether, and Monda kept her under. I opened the abdomen with a couple of nursing orderlies to help, removed the dead baby and placenta, stopped the bleeding, and cleared most of the blood out of the abdomen. I then started sewing up the tear in her uterus. I was nearly finished when all of a sudden, she stopped breathing. Only a few minutes before, her blood pressure had been good. It became obvious that she had a reaction to one of the blood transfusions. We had administered medicine to anticipate this possibility, but perhaps the bleeding and shock contributed to her death as well. We were all crushed. I couldn't help but think if Giles had been there, she would have made it.

Her husband was devastated when we told him. Here were a man and woman whom we all loved. He was a partner in ministry. He told us that she had been having pain for a couple of days. If only they had told us then, Giles could have operated. I felt terrible. Although there was nothing I could have done differently with our limited equipment, I blamed myself for something that I couldn't have prevented. It was a nightmare for everyone on the station.

I finally got home at 9:30 A.M. I walked to the front door, and Gilesie met me and vomited everywhere. I cleaned him up, ate a quick breakfast, extended the child care, and went back to the hospital. A dazed Pastor Sithole told us that he would send someone to Gatooma to inform her family to come immediately so that she could be buried. We usually buried those who died right away since we had no way to properly embalm a body, but he insisted that he would have to wait, even though the heat in February was stifling. I decided it would be best to shoot a couple of quarts of formaldehyde into the body cavities, just in case it took a while for the family to come.

By the time I returned home at midday to check on the boys and my helper, I was weary and still overcome with grief.

Chapter 7

A white man was sitting in our living room. Occasionally he came to Sanyati to oversee some of the construction. He wanted me to serve him tea, and I was in no mood to be a hostess. After serving tea, he kept talking and talking while I had more pressing things to attend to like helping my friends wash and dress Mrs. Sithole's body. I was grieving, and he was chatting about insignificant and irrelevant things, with no knowledge of what had happened. Finally he left, and I ran out to the garden to cut some flowers. Monda and I hurriedly walked to Pastor Sithole's house with the flowers and stayed while the body was being laid out. It broke my heart to see Pastor Sithole. We had received word that Giles had been delayed in Gatooma, because our truck needed repairs. Therefore, he had no idea about Mrs. Sithole's death.

Mrs. Sithole's sister managed to arrive later that day, so they proceeded with the funeral late that afternoon. Since none of the missionary men were on the compound, and Mr. Nyathi had died, Pastor Sithole asked Monda, Mary, and me to say a few words at the funeral. He was not up to speaking. It was one of the hardest things I've ever been asked to do. After the service, everyone walked down to the place where we had started a cemetery. This was the second funeral and burial at the station. A grave had been dug, and the coffin was placed in the hole. In my head I heard the dirt thud each time a shovelful was tossed in. The flowers I had cut and tree branches were placed on the filled grave just before dusk.

After the funeral, I went back to the hospital to check on two patients; but by the time I arrived, there were six. One was a little girl about four years old with a badly swollen face and neck and a membrane in her throat. As soon as I saw it, I knew it was diphtheria. Since we didn't have an isolation ward at that time, a diagnosis of diphtheria was catastrophic. I had to put her in the washroom where there was no electricity and rig up a kerosene lantern so that I could prepare for a tracheotomy, if needed. With the autoclave not working, all the equipment had to be sterilized in the pressure cooker on the Coleman stove.

By the time I finished with all the patients, it was 8:00 P.M. Mary had Gilesie and David over at the Kratz house while also looking after Becca and the new baby, Owen Kratz. Dot had been at the hospital doing our needed lab work. Giles finally got home at midnight, and I had to help him unload. It was 2:00 A.M. before we got in bed, and I had been up about 23 hours with only 4 hours of sleep the night before. But I had to tell him everything since he had not heard about the tragedy. I wept and wept. It was 4:00 A.M. before we finally fell asleep.

I had many questions for God but was too exhausted to voice them. People were coming to Christ in Sanyati, and we envisioned new areas where the gospel needed to go. Why were all these bad things happening? Weren't we doing what God called us to do? Why didn't Mrs. Sithole survive the surgery? I did my best. I prayed that God would keep her alive. We were being obedient. Passages in Job kept coming to my mind. Hadn't Pastor Sithole even preached from Job during Pastor Nyathi's funeral? For the next few weeks,

Chapter 7

I began to wonder why we had come. Even during a church service one morning as I was trying to keep the rain off the boys and stuffing jelly beans in their mouths, I still heard the enemy taunting me about why we were in Africa. I needed some kind of encouragement from God.

CHAPTER 8

A Thousand Times *Yes*

BY THE TIME we had been at Sanyati Baptist Hospital for two years, blessings were overflowing. Our missionary personnel count was increasing. Bill and Blanche Wester and Sam and Ona Jones had been appointed. Then we got word that Tom and Mary Small would be appointed, and that Marvin and Mary Ellen Garrett would join our mission after transferring from Nigeria. Clyde Dotson had finished the translation of the Ndau Bible, bringing to a close 13 years of labor in perfecting this translation. Trips were being made into unreached areas. Several village schools had been set up. Seminary classes had been started in Gwelo (Gweru). Many baptisms had been recorded in Southern Rhodesia, even in areas where we had no missionary personnel stationed. The hospital and school were growing. More and more patients were coming.

Especially exciting was that I was expecting again. As the oldest of seven Gibson girls, I had no experience with baby boys. Now after we had two beautiful boys, we were hoping for a baby girl this third time. However, the heart rate stayed in the slower range of normal throughout my pregnancy, so I knew the baby was another boy.

Gilesie and David were growing like weeds, and we were relieved because they were rarely sick. Other than Gilesie's eating of some wild mushrooms that he pulled up, and my having to pump his stomach, we had a pretty good track record for keeping them safe and healthy. The boys made me laugh. One day, Gilesie pointed to his rear end and said, "Nani, I want a tail." Trying to keep a straight face, I leaned down and said, "Little boys don't have tails; animals have tails." He replied, "My Dixie dog and bunny rabbit have tails, Nani." And that was the end of that conversation. If his animals had tails, he could too. At least he thought so.

Besides raising the boys, Giles and I stayed busy. I had no time for morning sickness. I tended to all pediatric cases at the hospital, supervised all the sewing of hospital linens and uniforms, helped keep the financial and historical hospital records, saw all patients when Giles was away, taught Sunday School, hosted guests, cooked, studied the language the best I could, and wrote correspondence for our family and the hospital. Giles had even more jobs than I. Looking back, I don't know how we did it, except by the grace of God. It was just the way it was, and I didn't think much about it.

But tragedy was something we never planned or had time for so when it happened, we were always caught by surprise. In March 1955, we had a terrible shock. On a Saturday afternoon,

Hattie Dotson was killed instantly in a head-on collision. She was on her motor scooter, had just turned onto a main thoroughfare in Salisbury where they had recently moved, and was well on her side of the road when a car swerved and hit her. She and the motor scooter were knocked about 80 feet down the road. Just the day before, Clyde Dotson, John Cheyne, Gerald Harvey, and David Lockard had come out to Sanyati for a called mission meeting. Eunice Harvey was pregnant with her second child, and Marie Cheyne was pregnant with her third, so both of those women had not come with their husbands. Hattie had decided to stay in Salisbury with their youngest girls who were still at home. Their youngest daughter, six-year-old Dorothy Joy, had been sick with scarlatina. Our called meeting had been long on Friday, actually lasting until 2:00 A.M. Saturday morning. Mr. Dotson was in a hurry to leave Saturday, which he did around 10:00 A.M. He had the carload of men with him to drop off in Gatooma. Just after he arrived in Gatooma, a stranger came to tell him that his wife had been in a serious accident. Gerald and Mr. Dotson immediately drove to Salisbury, only to find out that Hattie Dotson had died at the scene. Gerald took care of all the details for the grief-stricken Mr. Dotson. We didn't find out she had died until late that evening when Gerald drove back to Sanyati to tell us.

Of course, I was just sick to hear of this tragedy. We went to bed about 3:00 A.M. Sunday morning, the morning that would have been Hattie's 50th birthday. Since Mr. Dotson seemed so fond of Giles, and they had made the trip to

Nyasaland together, we all felt that Giles should go back to Salisbury with Gerald Sunday morning. Monda and Mary went too, to help with the Dotson children. The Kratzes decided to go to Salisbury also, so I was left to hold down the fort at Sanyati. I hated to miss the funeral on Monday, but someone had to be there for clinic and the hospital, and I was "it." So much was going through my mind. I couldn't imagine how Clyde Dotson was feeling and what would happen to him and the children. His three older girls were in the States, and his only son was in the army in Hawaii.

While everyone was in Salisbury, I admitted 3 very sick patients with malaria. One was a six-year-old girl who was terribly anemic, unconscious, and had cerebral malaria. I did everything I could, including blood transfusions. Giles and Gene got home at midnight on Monday after the funeral. Immediately, Gene had to collect a woman who was bleeding due to a miscarriage. Over the next two days, I prayed for the little girl with malaria to get better. On Thursday, she woke and had improved. The Lord answered my prayer. That same day, 12 more people had positive malaria tests; 3 of them required blood transfusions. Then 2 boys came in with bad fractures. One had been kicked by an ox, breaking both bones of his right leg. The other boy broke both bones of his left arm after falling from a tree. Since Monda was still in Salisbury helping Mr. Dotson with the children, my workload was harder, but the poor man needed all the help he could get. He was just beside himself about what to do without his wife.

By the end of the week, Giles couldn't wait to go out to the village schools with John Cheyne and escape the stress of the hospital and thoughts of the funeral. God encouraged my husband when about 75 people decided to follow Christ after he and John preached. More and more people were hearing the gospel and responding. And God was working out His plan for more missionary personnel and African leaders to answer His call to go to the unreached.

The next few months were a blur. It was decided that Mr. Dotson would move to Umtali to carry on work that had been started there. The Westers came to Sanyati to study language, but they would take over the work in Salisbury since Mr. Dotson had moved. The first GA convention was held at Sanyati, and the GA manual that Betty Bowlin and I wrote had been translated into ChiSezuru and Sindebele. Other babies were born to missionary personnel in 1955, including one baby who developed meningitis a few days after her birth at Sanyati, which I fortunately diagnosed early. Later it was discovered that she had a heart murmur that disappeared when she was five. Also, Martha Cheyne, David Kratz (Dot developed spinal meningitis just after delivery), and my own little boy were born.

When my labor started, I knew something wasn't right. Giles, of course, would deliver the baby, but he discovered that our son was in the "military" position, in which the baby's head was not flexed, and the face was turned anterior instead of the normal posterior. This abnormal presentation caused a longer and more difficult delivery since the head did not flex normally for delivery. The results could have been disastrous, because a presentation like this usually ends up being delivered by C-section. Two of my national friends remained seated in the hallway, praying for me and the baby as the painful hours passed. Finally, Robert Gordon Fort arrived "sunny side up" on October 15, 1955. We knew the stress of the delivery could have killed him or damaged his brain. God did take care of Gordon and me.

Gordon was a strong-willed baby. His dad reminded him for many years that he was too strong-willed to bend his neck, even to be born! (On many of Gordon's birthdays, Giles would ask Gordon to put his chin down, fully flexing his neck, and would say, "See, Gordon, you could have bent your head down, but you refused even to be born! You were even then determined and stubborn!")

We had a lot to be thankful for on Thanksgiving Day 1955. The mission dinner was held at our house but just as we were about to sit down to eat, John arrived announcing that the date had been moved up for the sailing of the ship taking Monda and Mary back to the States for furlough. In fact, he said that they had to pack and leave that very night to take the train to the ship hours and hours away in South Africa! There was never a dull moment at Sanyati.

I did reflect on the many things to be thankful for the next day. Even though we had lost Hattie Dotson, and we all truly missed her, God had blessed. By the end of the year, the Sanyati Baptist Church building was under construction. Already, there were nearly 200 members. Pastor Sithole, who had lost his own wife and baby, was the faithful pastor. He also was preaching at seven preaching points with more than 400 in attendance. I was thankful for the new x-ray machine. And by the end of the year, we had seen nearly 6,000 outpatients and just over 900 inpatients.

We were worried about Dot Kratz, who developed early signs of meningitis. A spinal tap revealed only a small number of shigellosis cells. These were thought to be a contaminant but just in case, we started her on medication and referred her to the infectious diseases hospital. They stopped the medicine but later restarted it. It took nearly a year for her to recover, and we considered it a near miracle that she did. We had to pack up all their belongings since they would not be able to continue missionary service—a real loss for us.

Monda was on furlough, and we were thrilled to hear that Polly Jackson, a registered nurse, had been appointed to serve at Sanyati. Another change in missionary personnel concerned the Garretts. Marvin had a bicycle accident and injured his back. He and his wife had to go to Dallas, Texas, for specialist care. We were blessed to have Gene and Jeannie Phillips, Logan and Ginny Atnip, and Dr. Vance to join our mission family in Southern Rhodesia just before we went on our first furlough. It had been postponed three times as we waited for Dr. Vance's arrival to take over the medical responsibilities at the hospital.

More than three years had gone by, and we were going back to the States. I was excited but also concerned about leaving the work at Sanyati. People had come to trust us as doctors. They graciously showed us appreciation by leaving melons from a prized patch, eggs, a chicken, and even a goat. Knowing most were very poor, I had to learn how to accept their gifts with true humility. Not only would I miss our patients, but I had truly come to love the girls in my Sunday School class and GA group. They were growing spiritually, and it blessed me to watch them. But nothing compared to seeing people come to Christ. The gospel of Christ was making a difference in Southern Rhodesia.

I knew, however, that as much as we loved the people of Africa, we had two new boys to introduce to our families in the States. My parents, sisters, and Giles's mother, sister, and brother were dying to see Gilesie again and meet David and Gordon. Two of my sisters were getting married in June 1956, and I was going to get back in time to attend both weddings. On our last night before leaving for furlough on May 27, Giles and I were walking home from the hospital talking about that day and the past three and a half years. That afternoon, a couple from Gokwe brought their little girl to the hospital. She was half-dead and severely anemic from chronic malaria. The river was finally dry enough to wade through to get to the hospital, so they brought her. We gave her a blood transfusion, medicine, and love from the Lord Jesus. Giles and I talked about the child and many of our other experiences since we arrived in Sanyati after our first time on The Road. Our hospital had been a small mud and pole hut. Our house was still under construction. We thought of our first patients who had to be transported to the hospital in Gatooma because our facility wasn't adequate at that time to treat severe cases. We remembered our first Christmas when the new hospital was opened, dedicated to the healing of broken, diseased bodies in the name of our Lord Jesus. As we entered the gate of our yard, our cup was full and running over with gratitude to the Lord for what He had done. We couldn't help but think of what we hoped for the future: a bridge over the river, better roads to have access to more people, student dorms for the school, a nursing school, and more personnel. Sanyati had become our beloved Sanyati.

If ever I knew what it meant to have two homes, I found out that summer we returned to the States. As I longed to see our families who lived in the States while I was in Sanyati, I yearned to be with our friends, to smell the rain and land, to see the brilliant stars, and to treat and minister to patients in Sanyati. In one term of service, we had fallen completely in love with Africa. I was overcome with gratitude that God had chosen us to live there.

Coming back to the States was an adjustment for our children. We left our home country when Gilesie was very young, and of course David and Gordon had not been born yet. On our first hotel stay since returning, Gilesie and little David saw the swimming pool with their father. David looked up and asked, "Daddy, ah theah any clockodiles in the liver?" Substituting *l* for *r* was common for David since he had learned that pronunciation from one of the African schoolgirls. Of course, David had never seen a swimming pool—it looked like a river to him. And he had been cautioned many times about the danger of crocodiles in rivers!

Giles and I worked at Charity Hospital in Monroe, Louisiana, in general practice and anesthesia during our year in the States. Medicine had advanced since we had left the States just three and a half years earlier, and we needed to catch up. This time around, we both knew that what we learned truly would save people's lives in Africa. We stuck to learning what was practical based on our experience. People we met were fascinated by us for being "bush" doctors, and there was always someone who wanted to interview us for a newspaper. Way more than once we were asked, "Do you really like living in Africa?" I did not have to think about my answer. It was always a thousand times, "Yes!" God had transformed my heart to cause it to pine for Africa when I was away.

In September of 1957, we headed back to Africa with our eyes wide open, knowing what to expect when we returned. We boarded a ship in New York with familiar friends and new friends, Bud and Jane Fray and their young family, who would be the answer to our prayers for eventual evangelistic work in Gokwe. Returning included the Garretts and Mr. Dotson, his youngest children, and his new, young wife named Ebbie (Kilgore). She was a nurse whom he had met and married several months earlier after returning to the States after Hattie had died. Ebbie was already expecting a child. I hoped she would be hardy enough to live in Umtali. As we left the New York City harbor, we passed right by the Statue of Liberty, and it hit me again that I was leaving my homeland, the land flowing with milk and honey, for more adventure in the needy Sanyati Reserve. The plan had been made that we would first stay a few weeks in Salisbury for intensive language learning. When we finally travelled on The Road to Sanyati, I knew I was coming back to our *musha*, our home.

In late January 1958, after only being back in Southern Rhodesia four months or so, we got word that the new Mrs. Dotson developed eclampsia, an attack of convulsions during pregnancy, about a month before her first baby was due. Matters became even more serious when she had kidney failure. Her condition spiraled downward so quickly that she died a short time after the birth of her stillborn baby.

Most of the mission family gathered at the graveside in the beautiful spot in Umtali where she was buried. Our hearts were broken once again for Clyde Dotson. He spoke with quiet faith in God in this time of heartache. Because he buried her in Africa, Ebbie's parents were distraught, which complicated the situation. It was terrible all the way around. Although he remained in Umtali for a while, he was granted a transfer to Gokwe to work but for one reason or another, he ended up in the remote area of Mtange.

One thing I've learned is true about God is that He gives and takes away (Job 1:21). Part of following His call is being able to accept this truth and say, "Blessed be the name of the Lord." And others had said yes to the call to help us such as Hugh and Becky McKinley, Buddy and Jean Albright (who eventually went to Northern Rhodesia), Dr. Sam and Ginny

Cannata — Ruby Shumate
Friends of

Cannata (Sam was a medical doctor coming to set up clinics in Gokwe), Milton and Barbara Cunningham, Bob and Thelma Beaty, Bennett and Wilma Thorpe, Alf and Elsie Revell (a British Baptist couple who partnered with our mission), and Zeb and Evelyn Moss (who eventually moved to Northern Rhodesia along with Tom and Mary Small). We had 30 missionaries in the newly renamed Central Africa Mission, 14 church plants, 18 schools, an African seminary, and our hospital. Nationals were starting churches on their own once hearing the gospel in places like Que Que (Kwekwe) and Gutu. Even though the floodgates were opened, the new general secretary of our mission board, Dr. Goerner, had bad news for us when he visited in February of 1958. Our mission would not be expanding into Northern Rhodesia or Nyasaland due to a lack of candidates. So we kept praying that Baptists would hear the plea, "Come over to Africa to help us."

The Good Shepherd

OUR BOYS THRIVED in Africa. They ran all over the place with other children after homeschooling. Gilesie had become Giles III overnight when he turned seven; David, the image of his father, at five was an intuitive boy. Gordon, never short for words and very much unlike our older two, solemnly assured me at the table one day, "Mama, you do not have any *little* boys anymore." Well, we would soon. I was expecting again, and of course, the slow heart rate promised me another boy. I decided I must not be suited for girls. Giles and I did our best to shepherd the boys whom God had given.

The concept of shepherding became real to me from watching shepherd boys tend to the family goats or listening to my favorite teacher at the Sanyati Baptist School, Mr. Jeri Muvindi. My life as a child was idyllic compared to the life of this dear friend. Jeri had a difficult childhood. His father had two wives, and he was one of the children of four from the second wife. Polygamy caused a lot of problems, particularly strife between the senior wife and the subsequent wives and between children of the different mothers. When Jeri's father died, the oldest son from the first wife treated him like a slave. He was forced to tend to his father's herds of goat and cattle that had been left to the oldest son. Beaten and punished for no reason, our friend was reduced to wearing a loin cloth, which embarrassed him.

Jeri was not allowed to go to school as he grew up because he was told that he was unworthy and less than human. But one thing about him, he was a good herd boy. When he was 15 years old, he had a chance to hear a sermon in the Dutch Reformed Church from a missionary doctor. This man of God preached from John 10 about Jesus being the Good Shepherd. He didn't grasp the truth yet about Jesus being a shepherd, but he determined that he would be one. He memorized John 10 from hearing it, because he could not read. He knew all his cattle by names such as Busvumani, Bandomu, Blace, and Venandi.

One day, his difficult brother gave him a small bag of corn kernels to sell so that he could buy clothes to cover his nakedness. He walked 25 miles to a store, but he didn't buy clothing, even though he desperately needed some. Instead he purchased a Bible and a songbook. He still couldn't read, but he held that Bible out and carefully turned the pages as he pretended to be the missionary doctor preaching from John 10.

When Jeri reached home, his mother and brother were angry that he did not buy himself clothing. He had no clothes that year except his loin cloth and a long vest. But the Spirit of God opened this young man to the gospel of Jesus as he recited the words of John 10 over and over. As a result, dressed in his limited clothing, he walked to one of the *kraal* schools of the mission and asked the principal to allow him to be a student. "Sir, take me in because of John 10."

He was given an entrance test but failed miserably. Eventually, when he was 17 and still could not read, the principal had mercy on him and accepted him as a student. He told me, "I had no friends but Jesus. Each day, I prayed with my Bible open, I think upside down; I did not know! I did poorly in school until Jesus opened my eyes to read. Then I did better and finally finished eighth grade when I was 22 years old." Jesus was Jeri's teacher.

Seven years after he became a Christian, Jeri became a teacher and preacher. He joined the Salvation Army, and then he went to teacher's training school. He became one of our teachers at the Sanyati Baptist School. Did Jeri hold a grudge against his older brother? Never. He prayed for him and desired to lead his lost brother to find the Good Shepherd. I was humbled by this man who was a picture of Christ to so many.

After 7 years at Sanyati, we were seeing the Shepherd bring many to Himself, even those we thought were the impossible ones. There were two old *ambuyas* in the women's ward; one was 80 years old and the other, a few years younger. Pastor Sithole shared the gospel story with them and much to our surprise, they both decided to follow Jesus. One said, "For a long time, we have worshipped many different things because we did not know what we should worship. Today in the hospital I heard of the one God and His Son, Jesus, and now I know whom I should worship. I want to follow Jesus." It was amazing to think that for all those years, those grandmothers lived in superstition and fear, seeking something in which to place faith and trust. They had never been to a church service, they had never heard a preacher, but their families brought them to the hospital where they heard the gospel.

Another woman, who was the respected and feared "rainmaker" at the Mopani village, brought her children to the hospital. She had not allowed them to be hospitalized in the past but one day, she reluctantly allowed us to admit her youngest child who was ill with pneumonia. Witch doctors' remedies had failed to cure him, so we were her last resort. The red blankets petrified her, but she was more frightened that her child would die. So at night, she superstitiously placed a black cloth over the red blanket that covered the child. How we prayed that this child might recover! We told the mother that many were praying and trusting in God to help her son recover, even as we gave him medicine and treatment. If he did get well, we knew it would be a real witness to many in the reserve. How we thanked God when he began to get better!

After he went home, a large number of relatives from across the river came to the hospital for medical care. They would never have walked the many miles to attend the church but because of the hospital, we were able to reach them with the news that Jesus died for them too. God was calling His children, His lost sheep.

The verses in John 10 came alive: "The sheep hear his voice; and he calls his own sheep by name and leads them out. . . . The sheep follow him, for they knew his voice. . . . I am the door of the sheep. . . . If anyone enters by Me, he will be saved. . . . I am the good shepherd. The good shepherd gives His life for the sheep." In my heart, there was a continuing sense of God's call on my life and that I was in the center of His will. As a pediatrician, I felt particularly called to pray for and administer God's love and healing touch to the young.

Hungry children were as many as the grains of sand in the dusty reserve. Almost every day my heart ached to see starved and half-starved little children. Constantly, I saw cases of severe pellagra, rickets, kwashiorkor, and anemia, all diseases caused by a lack of protein, vitamins, or iron in the diet. When children suffered from those diseases, an epidemic like measles could nearly wipe out a generation. Indeed, an epidemic broke out, and many children died. Were my boys more special to the Lord because they had food, plenty to wear, and doctors for parents? No. Not at all. I knew that we were no better or more deserving than any of our African neighbors. In the face of such marked contrast, we were acutely aware of His marvelous goodness to us and our own great unworthiness. We were determined to follow God's call because of the blessings we had been given and because of our love for the Lord. I was aware that a lifetime of dedicated service to our Lord was pitifully inadequate to repay Him. I could only kneel in deep gratitude to Him. I had the guidance of the Good Shepherd in all His richness and beauty. Sadder than a child starving from lack of food was the person starving in his soul from lack of salvation that comes from trust in the Lord Jesus Christ.

Our new colleagues, Bud and Jane Fray, became kindred spirits in the ways of the Lord on a deep level. From the moment we sailed with them on the ship for our second term of service and their first term, Jane and I bonded immediately. Giles delivered their son, Jeff, as I stood right behind Jane's head, coaching and holding her hand while she screamed for ether! Six months later, that baby was diagnosed with polio. We had many long prayertimes over the sick child. I had no idea at that time how Jane would reciprocate during my need sometime later. Then when Jeff had malaria, and I was pregnant again, we got him through.

Jane and I taught our children together and became close sisters in the faith. She taught English and geography while I stuck to math and science. Just like our children, our favorite time was recess. While they played, we drank iced coffee together and talked up a storm. Other missionary women were certainly my friends, but sometimes I felt that maybe a few of them were intimidated because I was a doctor. Certainly my colleagues were wonderful people whom I have the greatest regard for even today. But Jane was special. I loved her children like mine, and she loved my boys like hers. Gregg, our fourth son, was born on November 30, 1959, when I was 36 years old. It seemed that Jane and I learned to be better mothers together.

Our Christian family of missionaries and African believers watched God bring many people to Himself at the end of a decade and the beginning of the 1960s, despite increasing racial strife in the area. Two more missionary couples, Ralph and Laverne Rummage and Carroll and Jackie Shaw, joined our mission. In 1960, Billy Graham and his team came to Rhodesia. Hundreds of Africans and Europeans attended the crusade in one location, something nearly unheard of in that day and time. One of our teachers from Sanyati even commented that he couldn't believe black and white came down to the platform together during the invitation after hearing the powerful messages delivered by Rev. Graham. Hundreds professed their newfound faith in Christ.

Things were really going well. Not only were people coming to faith right and left, pastors were being trained at the seminary, work was finally opening up in Northern Rhodesia and Nyasaland, and the chapel and obstetrical block were opened at Sanyati. It was basically a happy time. I had no issues with discontentment, doubt, and certainly not despair. But I was tested not long after, and my husband and my friends, Jane and Mrs. Nyathi, would see that I wasn't as strong as everyone thought. I had to choose which part of John 10:10 I would focus: "The thief does not come except to steal, and to kill, and to destroy" or "I have come that they may have life, and that they may have it more abundantly." It was time to go back to God's school to learn about abundant life and overwhelming joy.

Grady

INCREASING RACIAL TENSION in the country in the early 1960s caused our mission to have to think about possibilities that we didn't want to consider. One of those was evacuation. The white people in the country wanted independence from the United Kingdom, and the Africans wanted independence from the whites. It made for a tenuous situation. Our mission had been warned by the government that there could be terrorist attacks by guerillas who had left the country to train in China under the Communists. Already a farm not many miles from us had been attacked. In one of the houses on our mission property, we stocked a locked closet with supplies, including food, guns, water, candles, lamps, and a shortwave radio. We were told to prepare ourselves to leave at a moment's notice.

I was concerned about what was happening in my beloved *musha*; I had a lot on my mind, especially being 38 years old and pregnant again. I was too old to be having babies.

I couldn't help but think of Matthew 2:19: "But woe to those who are pregnant and to those who are nursing babies in those days!" After Giles and I prayed about the situation one night, he reassured me with Psalm 4:8: "I will both lie down in peace, and sleep; For You alone, O LORD, make me dwell in safety." Giles was just like that. He didn't stress or worry but had a dependence on God that settled me. Although throughout the 1960s reports of attacks were made on buses, stores, and government employees, somehow we felt safe and knew our friends would warn us if we were ever in danger because of the color of our skin. We did hear of persecution of national Christians and pastors being tortured for teaching and speaking about the white man's God instead of following the African traditional beliefs. Perhaps our lives were in danger during this time, but we were blessedly unaware of it.

With two new doctors, Dr. Sam Cannata and Dr. Frances Greenway, who came in 1959, we watched our health ministry expand. Gokwe was wide open to spread the gospel and treat the sick. An airstrip had been built under the direction of Bud Fray at Sanyati, so we now had the capability of treating people at remote clinics that we had set up and bringing emergency cases to Sanyati. Drought had plagued the land, so hunger was common, which brought on a host of diseases for children. I remember standing by the bed of a sick child during that time. Many were sick or dying. I tried to assure the mother of God's love, but I thought she must wonder how I could possibly understand. I had never seen one of my sons dying from malnutrition. What did I know of suffering?

The day I went into labor on July 20, 1961, my life changed. Giles delivered our fifth son, the fourth son of ours to be born at Sanyati Baptist Hospital. As soon as he handed the baby to me, I knew something wasn't normal. He was just too flaccid. Several times I measured his head size, which was almost normal. My doctor mind immediately said, "Down syndrome," but my mother heart refused to talk about it. Giles didn't say anything either. Grief, disappointment, confusion . . . I felt all those things. I was sorry for myself. Having a Down's baby in 1961 was not as accepted as it is today. I was despondent.

Even my friend Jane didn't know what to say at first. In fact, my missionary colleagues, I think, were afraid to say anything at all. The next couple of days, I was basically alone with my baby. With me out of commission, Giles was taking care of what would have been my cases. It gave me plenty of time to see my pride for what it was—ugly. I was a doctor, who graduated summa cum laude, and married a doctor. I had followed God to the wilds of Africa. I already had four healthy, fine young boys. I had a successful ministry. I could survive in primitive conditions. I was loved and respected. Oh, how God kept trying to tell me that I was nothing without Him. It was not a pretty picture, but God was gently telling me to get over myself.

Three days after Grady's birth, Giles came in and sat in the rocker in the bedroom while I stood by the baby's cradle. He said, "We have got to talk to the Lord about this, Wana Ann." I didn't particularly want to talk to the Lord about anything. I was numb. My heart was broken. But Giles bowed his head and asked God to make us teachable in this difficult situation. My pride was completely and utterly exposed in my heart, and I was wholly vulnerable.

Later that day, two of my national friends came to my house. "We know your baby is not all right," said one of them. "No," I admitted quietly to them . . . and to myself. "He's not all right." The other said, "It is our Christian custom when people are sick or in sorrow to come and pray with them. So we have come to pray with you." I felt the love of God for me through the love and care of those dear women. I bowed my head, and with tears streaming down my face, I listened as they prayed in their language for our baby, me, and Giles.

God had mercy on me in that moment. Grady's condition was not going to change but mine was. I will never forget the wonderful, comforting presence of the Holy Spirit in my bedroom that afternoon. God assured me that He was going to make our experience with Grady in our family "all right." Those precious women and God's Holy Spirit ministered to me.

What I thought would be my suffering turned out to be a deeper walk with the Lord and an understanding of abundant life and joy. Giles's prayer that God would make us teachable was answered. I was afraid that I wouldn't know how to be a mother of a child with special needs. I was afraid of failure. I turned to the Father to help me, because I knew that Giles and I needed His direction on how to raise our new son. Our boys, of course, didn't have the initial reaction that we did. They were totally in love with their new baby brother. Our mission family learned a lot too, and Grady became everyone's favorite. And why wouldn't he be? He was a bundle of love from the get-go.

What could have turned into a dark depression was illuminated by a ray of sunshine named Grady. As the months went by, Giles and I decided we would not hide him from the traditionally superstitious people, and we would treat Grady the same as his brothers, as far as possible. His brothers treated him just like each other as well.

From the time Grady was a toddler, Gordon would sit at the dinner table and egg Grady on to do something he shouldn't, such as call Gregg "Geg-a-teez Socrates Miller." Don't ask me why! Of course, this name infuriated Gregg, and Grady would grin and say it repeatedly. Gordon thought I didn't know the shenanigans he was up to, but I did. Since Gordon was the instigator when he was a young boy, I always had my eye on that enthusiastic and imaginative child. I'll never forget on our furlough when Gordon was in first grade, his teacher kept on asking him to tell a story about Africa. To Gordon, Africa was home, and he didn't know any impressive stories. Well, he finally placated her by sharing a report to the class that while in Africa, his daddy had gone to the front door and found a big lion there. He said his dad ran, and the lion came dashing through the house and through the back door, not harming anyone. Of course, Gordon was making this up, but the whole class, including the teacher, believed it! They wanted a "real African story," so Gordon told one!

While Gordon was a fun-hearted prankster with Grady, Gregg helped me take care of our fifth son, which was an appreciated contribution. One thing is true—our family loves Grady. Everyone does.

A few months after Grady was born, Giles, a Missionary Aviation Fellowship (MAF) pilot, Ted, and a visiting missionary, Dr. David Drake, of the Evangelical Alliance Mission (TEAM), left early in the morning to fly to Sesame, one of our new stations in Gokwe where the Frays had moved. Giles and Ted were going to pick up Willy, a nursing orderly there, and fly on to the medical clinics in Tonga areas of the Gokwe Reserve. Flying was expensive, but it was the only way to treat patients in those remote areas. It was a Monday, and I had a heavy schedule with working at the hospital that morning, house guests all day, the week of prayer program that afternoon, and dinner at my house for guests. After dinner, we had the regular, weekly prayer meeting at our home. As the refreshments for the group, I served my "wonder" cobbler, aptly named by me because it was a wonder I had time to do it! (See recipe on p. 199.) Of course, on top of all that, I had to check on our boys who were with my helper. Giles was supposed to be back in time for dinner but told me that he would keep me informed by our shortwave radio during each scheduled check time. He had no idea if they might have to spend the night at the Frays' home if the patient load at the two clinics was more than they could handle in a day.

At the noon check, I talked with Jane at Sesame. Jane was concerned because she had contacted Ted as he was landing from flying Dr. Drake to Nenyuka from Semchembu. Ted said that he would soon be taking off from Nenyuka with Giles and Willy but had not come back on the air. Bud came on the radio and reassured me that they were probably still seeing patients and would contact Jane later. Concerned, I agreed and arranged to talk to Jane again at 5:00 P.M. I toted Grady around while I continued with the things I needed to do that afternoon.

At 5:00 P.M., I contacted Jane. She said there had been no contact and that she had called the police at a village about 30 miles away from them. Even in a Land Rover, the police said that it would take them until midnight to reach what they called Tongaland. Bud said that perhaps they had gotten stuck in the mud on the crude air strip. Jane and I arranged for another radio check at 1:00 A.M. With more concern this time, I reluctantly went home to feed our house guests and our boys and then hosted the prayer meeting.

The boys were sleeping, the guests had gone off to bed, and finally at 11:00 P.M., I set my alarm clock to awaken me just before 1:00 A.M. Two of our two-year young missionaries (journeymen) surprised me by coming to join me at the radio shack at 1:00 A.M. when I made the call. Much to our dismay, we got the bad news that the plane had crashed. A cold chill ran from my head to my toes. Then we were told that everyone was OK and that the police in the Land Rover had found them. They were on their way back to Sesame in the Land Rover. There had been good rains, and the grass on the strip was higher than usual. Also, the strip had not been cut according to schedule. Landing had not been difficult but when they attempted the takeoff, they failed to clear the trees at the end of the strip, and the plane turned upside down. They complained that the only pain experienced was when they unfastened their seat belts and their heads hit the top of the plane when they were released! The local chief let them stay in a hut until someone came for them.

Since Grady's birth, God had been teaching me much about trusting Him. My natural tendency was to start thinking the "what ifs" such as: What if fire had broken out after the crash? What if Giles had been killed? Who would help me raise these boys, especially Grady? But somehow, because of Grady, I didn't dwell on these thoughts. God was teaching me so much about being thankful in all circumstances as stated in 1 Thessalonians 5:18: "In everything give thanks; for this is the will of God in Christ Jesus for you."

Giles returned no worse for the wear except for many mosquito bites. Their seat belts had held them securely in the plane when it flipped, and it was amazing that they walked away from the crash with no major injuries. I was relieved that Giles didn't get malaria later due to the bites.

I have Grady to thank for realizing that God has everything under control. He doesn't need me to tell Him, the sovereign God, what is best for me. Grady also taught me much about worship. Grady made our whole family better people, and I'm sure he affected others in the same way. Any time someone came to my house to play our piano, like Jane or in the mid-1960s, Nurse Mary Louise Clark, a big smile would light up on

Grady's face as he rocked in beat with the notes. His favorite hymns were and probably still are "Victory in Jesus" and "Amazing Grace." When he was older, we bought him a record player, and he'd sit and listen, smiling the whole time. Music was a part of our family, just as it had been in my own growing-up years. My sons may have been ruffians running all over the mission station during their free time but in the evenings, I tried to teach them to be gentlemen. Clean and dressed nicely, they came to the supper table each night. I often had candles lit on the table, and we listened to orchestral music directed by the Italian conductor Mantovani. We all got a kick out of how Grady had such an appreciation of music. At the table, elbows were forbidden. But that was hard to teach Grady. He would just grin when I'd tell him. To this day, I don't know anyone who smiles more than our fifth son.

Our uniquely different sons were gifts from God. We were firm with them when necessary but for the most part, we didn't have to resort to harsh discipline. Sending them to their rooms when they misbehaved seemed to work. Because we were a family of strong individuals, my husband and I decided that if we had a disagreement and it was over something with factual evidence, we would look up the information to settle the matter. If it were a disagreement over an opinion, each was entitled to his own as long as it was expressed as such. Giles, being the oldest son, sought independence. David was concerned about excelling in everything and following the rules. Gordon was mischievous but when he fully surrendered to the Lord, he had a complete turnaround. Gregg was a true

African who mastered the language, whose frame of reference was completely based on Africa, and who became fully accepted by the people. And Grady was positive, happy, and had a trusting, childlike faith. All gave their lives to Christ, which was the most important answer to prayer to us.

Having Grady limited my time away from home and affected my hospital commitments. It became increasingly evident that Giles and David needed more schooling than I could give them, so when Grady was about 1½ years old, we enrolled Giles and David into a boarding school in Bulawayo, 250 miles away. Giles was almost 12, and David was nearly 10.

I drove them to the boys' hostel at Hillside Primary School. After greeting the headmaster, and a few of the teachers, I paid the necessary fees. Then we walked up the stairs to the younger boys' dorm. The matron agreed our boys could stay together at first; later Giles would move into the middle boys' dorm. She assured me that all her boys adjusted fine, and I didn't need to be concerned. There was a mist in a pair of brown eyes and a pair of blue eyes and too much in my own to linger. I felt like my heart was being wrenched out of my chest. We quickly hugged. I ran down the stairs and out to the car.

Two years later, I took Gordon to the same school. Each time was not easier. And I knew that Grady would need special education. By the time Gordon went to school, Grady had only started saying a few words. His progress was painstakingly slow, and I had to accept the hard fact that I was not qualified to teach a child with Down syndrome to his fullest potential. There was no help in or near Sanyati. Once the three boys were away at school, I served primarily as a mom and oversaw Gregg's homeschooling, but I also was the pediatric consultant, supervisor of the care of premature babies, assistant for administering anesthetics, and the accountant for the mission station. I was not superwoman and needed a solution to the situation.

Some people, even our colleagues, probably thought that because of Grady, we had an excuse to go back to the States and resign missionary service. However, Giles and I were not released from God's call on our lives. The Lord promised to bless 100-fold and that His grace was sufficient. We would not abandon or personally redirect the call of God on our lives. While we were on furlough in 1962, and we were introducing Gregg and Grady to our family, perhaps even our family thought we should stay home. My mother and Giles's mother loved on their five grandsons and never questioned our call. I'm just so glad that MeMe got to meet them all since I received a telegram after we returned to Rhodesia in 1963 that my mother had died of cancer. Did I have to struggle with feelings of self-imposed guilt that I had missed my mother's last years? Of course. I had to lean on the promises of God and cherish the trip she made in 1959 to Africa to stay with us several weeks. I was grateful to my father for sending her for that visit.

When Grady was seven, a place became open at Sir Humphrey Gibbs Training Centre, a boarding school for special-needs children in the same town where Giles, David, and Gordon went to school. (Once in high school, our three older boys attended Milton High School in the same town.) Grady wanted to be a "big boy" like his three brothers. We visited the lovely school and made the difficult decision to enroll Grady. Many people prayed for his transition when he started school, and God's mercy and grace helped us all to release Grady into God's care at this place where Grady could have the opportunity to progress.

A two-year-term missionary journeyman came to Sanyati to homeschool Gregg until he went to a boarding school in Gwelo when he was around ten years old. I never envisioned that we would have to send all our sons away to school. Perhaps I avoided thinking about it. The boys thrived at their schools in academics, sports, and leadership. And Grady, with his cheerful disposition, bloomed far more than we even hoped.

During school holidays—three a year—things came alive again around the Fort house. I tried not to focus on the time we didn't spend together. For the sake of our boys, we had to make hard decisions so that they would get a good education and have the best opportunity possible to be who they were meant to be. The four older boys and Giles went on a hunting trip every year while I stayed home with Grady and attended to the hospital. To this day, I'm sure each of them will tell you those were some of the best times of their lives with their beloved father in the bush of Africa. After the holidays, the house was too quiet, empty, and tidy. I ached for them.

Following God includes sacrifice. For us, it was sending our boys off to school at young ages. We committed to write weekly letters, visit them when we could, and most important, stay on our knees for them. We prayed that our children would never become idols in our lives but that our worship was always directed to the Father. Even though it was not easy, God was faithful to see all of us through it. We weren't perfect parents. But we did our best to obey God; our children belonged to Him. We would not demand from God the ownership of our children.

CHAPTER 11

The New Normal

THE GLORIOUS PURPLE of the jacarandas in bloom was followed by the brilliant, red flamboyant trees—the aroma of the blossoms sweet in the air. The grass was green due to early rains, hopefully a foreshadowing of more rain to end the drought. Everyone felt better in the rain. Clyde Dotson had married again; this third time to a Finnish nurse, Anneli, who had worked in South Africa. New career and associate missionaries came to Rhodesia in the 1960s including Herb and Jackie Neely, Ira and Georgia Singleton, James and Nema Westmoreland, Dr. Lorne and Virginia Brown, John and Florence Griggs, Donna Stiles, Franklin and Re Milby, Mary Louise Clark, Rob and Eloise Garrett, Jimmy and Charlotte Walker, Ray and Billie Bell, Jerry and Barbara Schleiff, Herb and Wanda Edminster, Bob and Mary Parker, C. W. and Vertie McClelland, Ed and Missy Moses, and David and Linda Coleman. Two-year missionaries also came, including

Patricia Lemonds, Linda Stringer, Veronica Wheeler, Connie Roediger, Janice Self, Margo Fallin, Mary Hubbard, Pam Kelley, and Lora Taylor. Some of the new personnel came to Sanyati, and we felt blessed.

Not only did we have new personnel but also we were able to open an isolation ward. Giles's mother, who was visiting us at the time, was the guest of honor who was asked to open the doors of the new ward for the first time. We also opened a new medical block. Not a day passed since the beginning of the hospital without prayer, devotions, Bible study, preaching, and witnessing led by our chaplain, Rev. Semwayo. Churches were being planted, and more and more people were coming to Christ. Everything seemed normal and positive, much to our delight.

But Rhodesia in the mid- to late-1960s continued to be a simmering pot of racial tension that would start boiling over in the 1970s with horrendous violence. We still had our storeroom with preparations in case of evacuation, but we did not entertain the thought that we really might be forced to leave. We continued in the happy place of routine medical work and evangelization. Life was too busy to think about the politics in the country. We had enough to think about with patients and bizarre religious beliefs.

One religious sect in Rhodesia was called the African Apostolic Church of John Maranke. This Shona man, who died in the early 1960s, had started the sect because he believed he was Christ's African apostle, even prophet, to bring salvation to Africa. His followers were taught to believe in a healing-and-exorcism ministry that negated the need for modern medicine. So it was very rare that we would have a patient come to us if he or she were an apostle of John, as we called them.

One day, a policeman came to investigate the death of four children in a *kraal* that was known to follow this strange sect. He took Giles with him where many children had died from a measles outbreak. Giles and the policeman were directed to an isolation hut near the riverbed built by the family. The hut was away from the cluster of huts in the *kraal*. Entering the dark hut, they saw several children on mats on the floor. Young Joseph, nine, was the most seriously ill. He had not taken water for two days. From what I understood, this sect believed that it was a sin to take medicine and if it were God's will for a person to recover, the person would recover without medicine. So when the children became ill, they put them in the hut and watched four of them die, although the hospital was only a few miles away.

Giles asked the family if he could take Joseph to the hospital. They consented because they believed their son would die anyway. It seemed little Joseph would die on the short trip to Sanyati, but Giles prayed all the way, "Lord, what a witness it will be of the love of God as we know your love if You will heal this child."

For days, Joseph's life lay between life and death. Medicine and fluids were given, and slowly we watched the boy come back to health. We marveled at his recovery. Giles accompanied the family back to their *kraal* with Joseph where he preached about the great God of love who wanted this boy to live so that His greatness could be known. The name of Jesus was glorified in the intense darkness of the village.

A father of another little boy being treated in our hospital was also a patient. He had a severe knee infection. The boy, Chisikwa, was severely malnourished. Chisikwa was near death many times but as we worked on this child, we witnessed to the father. Many, many times the father looked us in the eyes and refused to believe in Jesus. But then he stood by the bed of a man who died. The next day, he talked to us about becoming a Christian.

We held our New Life for You crusade in September 1968 in different locations in Rhodesia, including Sanyati. A well-known African American pastor, Dr. S. M. Lockridge from San Diego, and 14 Americans partnered with our mission and national Baptist leaders, particularly Rev. Abel Nziramasanga, the president of the country's Baptist Convention. Rev. Nziramasanga was the father of Ralph, the little baby who was my very first patient in 1953. During the crusade, crowds came to hear Dr. Lockridge because of his skin color, his large frame, and his gray hair. When the revival meetings moved to the Gokwe Reserve, a knock came at my bedroom window at 3:00 A.M. I heard someone give a message with a sob, "Come and help. Nurse Lillian is about to die!" Giles had been at the hospital most of the night already tending to this nurse who had given birth to a stillborn the evening before. Apparently she was hemorrhaging and needed us immediately.

We hurriedly dressed and walked up the path to the hospital. We had known this woman since she was a little girl when we first came to Sanyati in 1953. Her mother had died tragically in childbirth and, as the eldest child, she had cared for younger brothers and sisters. We had watched her grow. Lillian was a good student, active in school and church. In fact, she was one of our first two GAs receiving Queen status. After completing school at Sanyati, she went to nursing orderly school and graduated with top honors. Then she came to work at our hospital. Her manner was quiet, she was efficient, and she cared for her patients. Lillian's Christian witness affected the work of the entire hospital staff. She had married one of our Baptist teachers in a beautiful wedding. And it was thrilling to hear the news of her pregnancy several months later.

I prayed the whole way up the path that God would spare her. Somehow, God gave me peace and through the nightmare hours that followed once I arrived at the hospital, God showed us His power in a series of events that could have no other explanation except that God is sovereign and omnipotent. Students, teachers, and a missionary gave blood willingly for her, more than a dozen pints. We had just gotten our first telephone installed at Sanyati, and we called the professor of obstetrics at the university's college of medicine in Salisbury. He was once a missionary in Nigeria, and he offered immediately to drive the 150 miles to help us. About 8:00 A.M. when he arrived, after driving on The Road, the hemorrhage, which had temporarily been under control, became profuse again. A hysterectomy was urgent. The doctor and Giles performed the surgery.

That afternoon, Lillian began bleeding again. We decided to attempt to contact the MAF pilot so that she could be flown to the Harare Hospital in Salisbury. The pilot was in Gokwe for the revival meetings and the usual clinic days. As one of our missionaries waited in the shortwave radio room tuned to the pilot's frequency, we prayed he would come on the air. As he departed from one of the clinics, he came on the air, the only time he had done so after a clinic for no apparent reason. The Holy Spirit had led him to check in.

By late afternoon, Lillian was transported to the Harare Hospital where a surgeon had to remove a huge blood clot. She was given more blood. Since her kidneys had failed, she was hooked up to their artificial kidney machine, the only one of its kind in Rhodesia at the time. For two weeks, Lillian required treatment on that machine before her kidneys recovered completely. When she seemed near recovery, she had a secondary hemorrhage requiring more surgery and four more pints of blood. In it all, God was present and healed.

The morning she flew back to Sanyati on the MAF plane was an extremely exciting day. As her husband said, "God performed a miracle when He healed my wife and let her live." Her own testimony was powerful. She said that while she was attending one of the revival services before being rushed to the hospital a couple of days later, she had recognized the need in her Christian life for greater spiritual depth. She yielded her life Him. Of course, God knew what she was about to go through and prepared her beforehand, as He always does. When she needed extra strength in Him, she already had been given it. It was a great tragedy that she lost her firstborn and would never have children, but she and her husband knew that God worked a miracle.

This was just one story that showed how partnership worked. Our Southern Baptist missionaries and missionary doctors worked with national Christians, MAF, other Christian doctors, volunteers, students, and Stateside churches as we sought to share the good news of Christ. And I knew that we couldn't survive without the many prayer partners we had in the States who constantly lifted us up to the Father. We received letters, and I wrote countless correspondence concerning prayer requests. Since my mother had died, I guess Giles's mother prayed more for us than anyone, but I also knew hundreds of people in churches, close friends, and family members who prayed regularly for my family.

One of my prayer requests was for me to always follow God's will. I often prayed Psalm 25:4–15:

> *Show me Your ways, O LORD; Teach me Your paths. Lead me in Your truth and teach me, For You are the God of my salvation; On You I wait all the day. Remember, O LORD, Your tender mercies and Your lovingkindnesses, For they are from of old. Do not remember the sins of my youth, nor my transgressions; According to Your mercy remember me, For Your goodness' sake,*

O Lord. Good and upright is the Lord; Therefore He teaches sinners in the way. The humble He guides in justice, And the humble He teaches His way. All the paths of the Lord are mercy and truth, To such as keep His covenant and His testimonies. For Your name's sake, O Lord, Pardon my iniquity, for it is great. Who is the man that fears the Lord? Him shall He teach in the way He chooses. He himself shall dwell in prosperity, And his descendants shall inherit the earth. The secret of the Lord is with those who fear Him, And He will show them His covenant. My eyes are ever toward the Lord, For He shall pluck my feet out of the net.

King David was a man who could pray heartfelt words. He waited expectantly for God. He confessed his sin and constantly asked for forgiveness. I wanted to be the kind of woman God could lead and have God's power to obey Him. I wanted to have His direction daily and a heart like His.

I had been a missionary doctor for 15 years. I was not the same person who sailed on the SS *Stella Lykes* in early 1953. Too much had happened, and God had taught me more than I could have imagined. I was still learning about life, being a wife and mother, and being a doctor and witness for Jesus. I was changing, and the world was changing. It was with great interest to me and Giles when just a country away in South Africa, Dr. Christiaan Barnard successfully completed the world's first heart transplant on another doctor, Dr. Phillip Blaiberg, in 1968. Incredible! I, a doctor, would never stand with a scalpel in my hand to cut out a man's scarred, inefficient heart and replace it with a new one. But I, a Christian doctor, could lead people to the Great Physician who can change hearts.

But I didn't know if Mairos, a new patient, would live long enough to soften his heart toward God.

CHAPTER 12

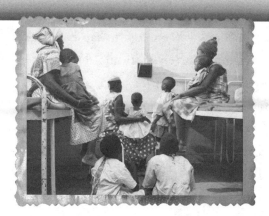

Worship

"I BAPTIZED MAIROS and his brother on Sunday," Bud Fray said to me in the hostel for our mission's missionary kids attending school in Gwelo. I had come to pick up Gregg, who impatiently waited at the car, eager to be on his way home for the weekend and his birthday. Bud had also come to the hostel to pick up his children. We had been good friends with the Frays ever since we traveled together from New York to Africa in 1957. For several years, the Frays had been stationed in Gokwe, and when we saw each other, we were happy to catch up on the news.

This word about Mairos was special news, and I stopped at the door on my way out to hear more. Gregg would have to wait a little longer. Memories of Mairos and his brother, Wiri, came flooding back. It began in August 1970. We had been very busy in clinic that morning at the hospital and were running late for lunch. Medical student Carole Nelson, a BSU summer missionary, and I were ready to leave for a 2:00 P.M. lunch when orderlies wheeled in a 34-year-old man on a stretcher. One look was enough to cause us to put down our things, resigning ourselves to an "early supper" instead of a late lunch.

The patient was only semiconscious. His face and arm muscles twitched, and his body was burning with fever. A quick examination revealed neck stiffness and pneumonia in the left lung. The man had been ill more than three weeks, but his family sought the witch doctor first. There were multiple cuts on his body made by the witch doctor to "release the poison." The illness began with fever and cough and progressed to marked weakness. After about five days, he complained of a headache and stiff neck. Then he became semiconscious, and the muscle twitch developed. The family lived many miles from any medical clinic or doctor but finally decided to send a man by bicycle to the hospital to ask for the ambulance. After the long trip, the patient had arrived.

Carole, eager to do the spinal tap, was surprised to see the milky fluid dripping from the needle. "I've never seen spinal fluid that looked like that," she said as she examined what was characteristic of pneumococcal meningitis. Linda Tiller, a lab technologist and BSU summer missionary, found pneumococci (bacteria) in the fluid. We began massive doses of penicillin in the intravenous drip.

After Mairos had been placed in the hospital bed and the initial treatments given, I talked with his brother about the seriousness of the illness. I explained that we would have had a better chance to help if they had come sooner. Then I asked if they were Christians. "Oh no," said Wiri, "we have never been to any church. I don't guess we have ever heard a sermon." Silently, my heart cried out to God to perform a miracle so that the desperately ill man would have at least an opportunity to hear the wonderful story of Jesus. At the bedside, we stopped to pray for Mairos to recover and for his brother to find new life in Christ. Wiri listened quietly. He said nothing as we left the room.

On rounds the next morning, I remarked to Carole, "You know, with pneumococcal meningitis, we must think about other things that could happen even if we kill the bacteria." Carole looked briefly at Mairos and said meaningfully, "I don't think you have to worry about residuals." She didn't think he would live. This man must survive, and I felt a fierce determination that he would. He could not come to the hospital and die without ever having a chance to know Jesus.

Several days passed. To our trained eyes, Mairos showed a few signs of improvement. His pulse was slower, his temperature not quite as high as on the first day, and the twitching was controlled. But his brother could not see much change. Mairos was still only semiconscious and thrashed around in bed when disturbed. He was fed by a tube and continued to be on intravenous fluids and medication.

Because, in general, Africans found it hard to understand any illness that lasted longer than a few days, the brother was sure the sickness would not respond to our medicine. Wiri decided the illness must be a disease caused by some unhappy family spirit. He believed that whatever was making the spirit disgruntled must be discerned so that atonement could be made on behalf of his brother. Also, Wiri probably was tired of having to take care of his brother. As I turned to leave the room after checking Mairos one morning, Wiri informed me that he had decided to take his brother home.

Well, I was livid. According to Nurse Mary Louise Clark, she said through much arm waving and my poor Shona, I convinced Wiri that his brother was *not* leaving the hospital. I explained that the disease was contagious. I assured him that if the witch doctor had not cured Mairos during the first three weeks of the illness, he certainly would not be able to help him any other time. I could not guarantee that his brother would recover, but I did tell him we were claiming God's power to help and were giving the correct medicines. We could only keep on praying and treating, and we were determined to do this *in the hospital*!

The vigorous declaration worked. No one ever mentioned again that it would be a good idea to take Mairos home. Days passed. The spinal fluid became completely clear. The main concern then was the persistent chest infection. After many weeks, the chest cleared completely, and Mairos gradually recovered. It did the staff good to see him sitting in a wheel-chair in the sunshine. He had lost considerable weight and was weak, but he was improving. Daily we thanked God.

Often we prayed for Mairos. And we shared with Wiri the concern that both men find Jesus as Savior while at the hospital. Daily, they heard the gospel over the loudspeaker that broadcast our chaplain's sermons. When he was able to leave Mairos, his brother attended chapel services. Later Mairos also attended in a wheelchair.

Chaplain Semwayo frequently visited and prayed for Mairos. He began to explain the way of salvation to Wiri and also to their uncle who came to see about the patient. Before Mairos went home, he, his brother, and his uncle decided to follow Christ. I was extremely happy and grateful to God.

When new believers left the hospital, the chaplain would write to the church nearest where they lived. In this instance, the letter went to the lay leader of the little Baptist church in Nenyuka, in Tonga country. There were not many believers in Nenyuka. Baptist work was begun there some years ago with a medical clinic. Response was slow. Finally, a few Christians met together. Bud baptized the first converts, and a little church was organized.

Later Chaplain Semwayo shared with us a letter from the lay leader in Nenyuka. He thanked the chaplain for writing about Mairos and Wiri and reported that they were faithfully attending services at the church in Nenyuka.

I was ecstatic when Bud told me that he had baptized Mairos. The purpose of the Sanyati Baptist Hospital was to heal the bodies and souls of men. The greatest privilege was to tell others about Jesus. Further fulfillment came when those who found Jesus returned to their villages to become part of a church there, witnessing to their own people.

Mairos, Wiri, and their uncle were only three of what was becoming an explosion of response to the gospel of Christ in the Sanyati and Gokwe Reserves. A revival had broken out about the same time as another measles outbreak. Not only were people responding to the gospel at the hospital and churches but also at our WMU associational meeting. Women were falling on their faces, asking God to forgive them for not being completely sold out to Him. Pastor Muvindi had been preaching. I was sitting under a tree as we listened to the sermon entitled "Jesus Is Lord" and then gathered with some women to pray during the decision time. All of a sudden, I heard a strange commotion in the crowd. A young woman began making loud noises and acting erratic. After all these years, I had never seen someone possessed by a demon, but I knew that was the situation with this woman. Had I not been accustomed to seeing the influence Satan had in the area, I would not have believed what was happening. She was screaming, moaning, and hissing while several ladies tried to control her. Pastor Muvindi explained that when the woman had come for prayer, the evil spirit began to speak from her. He asked me to pray for her to be delivered.

I was nervous, so I asked the Holy Spirit to take control and pray through me. Praying in the Shona language with unusual ease, I felt God's Spirit intensely, both within the room and within myself. As I prayed, others joined in, claiming the power of the Lord Jesus Christ to cast out the demon and free this tormented woman. Pastor Muvindi then held a Bible against the woman's forehead and demanded, "In the power of the blood of Jesus Christ, you leave!"

At that, the voice cried out from the woman, and she suddenly became limp and quiet. When the incident was over, the calm woman told us that she had been possessed by the spirit since a child. She wanted to follow Jesus. I saw the power of God against the evil spirit world, which seemed to become more common as the situation in Rhodesia became more politically volatile. Not long after this incident, I was asked to pray for another demon-possessed woman during another weekend convention.

Thinking about Mairos and these demon-possessed women coming to Christ, I couldn't help but think back to one of the first Africans I had the privilege of leading to the Lord. There was a student named Sophie Chironga at the Sanyati school who suffered from ridicule because of her hunched back. Her depression over it troubled me, and my heart grew tender toward this girl who believed she was under a curse that caused her deformity. But I knew that God looked at the heart rather than outward appearance, so I began to seek her out.

I needed help making the bed linens for the hospital, one of my many jobs throughout the years. I decided to teach Sophie so that we could spend time together and so that she could be gainfully employed. It didn't take her long to learn how to sew on the manual treadle sewing machine. And she was good. Her confidence built when others began noticing her for excellent work rather than her hunched back.

I assured her that God loved her unconditionally. As she heard the gospel numerous times, she was drawn to Jesus. I was thrilled when she told me that she wanted to follow Christ. That day, Sophie became a Christian.

After she completed school, a young Christian man fell in love with Sophie and proposed to her. She couldn't believe that God would lead a man to spend the rest of his life with her. And she told me how wonderful it was to know that she was perfect in God's sight and in that of her new husband.

And of course, there was Chief Whozhele, who was probably in his mid-50s at the time and had been one of the chiefs since we had arrived in Sanyati. His people had been moved truckload after truckload by the Rhodesian government in 1949 from the Kwekwe area to Sanyati, Chief Neuso's area. Although Chief Whozhele was friendly toward our mission and often attended special services on the station, all of us had been praying that he would become a follower of Jesus. One day when he was ill, and a patient in the hospital, he was refusing to eat. God led me to visit him, armed with a freshly baked apple pie and prayer. Four young men were in the room when I asked if I might give him some pie. They agreed but warned that he might not eat it. First, I prayed and felt the presence of God's Spirit. Then I fed the chief *all* of a big slice of pie, which he obviously enjoyed. The men watched with amazement!

I began treating him for his illness and when he recovered, I talked to him personally about Jesus. His heart was ready, and he and four male relatives in the room all decided to give their lives to Christ. We prayed together. Later he testified before a group, "I know that at one time people wondered if I would be able to stand before them ever again. I thank all the people who prayed for me. God gave His power so that I could continue to live here on this earth. I trust the doctors, but I trust God because He has the great power." (Interestingly enough, this chief is around 100 years old now. For several years, Dr. Mark and Angie Byler have served at the Sanyati Baptist Hospital on a salary basis. In 2011, Mark wrote, "There was an anonymous letter left at the hospital that I should be removed, and Chief Whozhele, while at the station meeting, stated that he did not want me removed and warned others against causing us problems.")

With so many turning to Christ, our mission expanded in the 1970s to accommodate the growth. New missionaries came: John and Anne Faulkner, Lois Calhoun, Betty Lynn Cadle, Phil and Judy Langley, Archie and Margaret Dunaway, Carolyn Roberson, Marvin and Bea Givler, Horace and Elizabeth Burns, Charles Campbell, Joey and Sylvia Williams, Bobby and Joahn Twiford, Gene and Beverly Kingsley, Karl and Susan Babb, Roger and Rita Bostick, Bob and Vicki Williamson, Elmon and Jody Woods, James and Paula Crossley (a Rhodesian couple who partnered with our mission), Curtis and Betty Dixon (temporarily reassigned from Angola), Quinn and Martha Morgan, Gary and Jo Tallman, Lolete Dotson (Clyde Dotson's daughter), Buck and Barbara Donaldson, and Ann Sliger—several whom were medical personnel.

Many journeymen, volunteers, and summer missionaries also came, some who were nurses or lab techs like Guy Lockart, Helen Roller, Charles and Gayla Corley (and son, Chip), and Terri Sutley. Giles and I were grateful for two new doctors at Sanyati—surgeon Maurice Randall and his wife, Shirley, and dentist John Monroe and his wife, Mary. Dr. Randall performed surgeries we had never done at the hospital before, and he became a partner to Giles in preaching on Sundays at the various preaching points. They would take care of patients needing immediate care early on Sundays while I taught Sunday School at the Mopani "line" nearest the station. (Houses were built in a line in the village; cattle were herded on one side and fields were on the other.) When I returned with the truck, Giles and Maurice would leave, while I stayed to care for emergencies. Dr. Monroe was not only a dentist, but also he was a first-rate surgical assistant.

And praise His name, in 1974 electricity came to Sanyati! No longer did we have to run generators and use kerosene lanterns. We had electricity 24 hours a day! God was answering prayer about many things. It was a harvest time in Rhodesia as people were turning to Christ during the tumultuous political environment. Many national young men were answering God's call to preach and were being trained at the thriving new Baptist seminary near Gwelo.

With all our sons off at school, including our oldest who was attending Texas A&M University, I had more time to be a doctor and spend time with people. But I really missed my boys, and I prayed that they would stay close to God. I wanted each of them to share his faith, not his parents' faith. More than anything, I wanted their relationships to the Lord not to be mediocre but vibrant. Putting son Giles on the plane to go to college, and later three other sons, made me realize that my life was often filled with the sharp pangs of good-byes. This caused me to pray harder for them and enabled me to rest in God. It became evident over the next few years that God was calling Giles and David to be medical doctors and Gordon and Gregg to be ministers of the gospel. I couldn't have been more delighted. And God had His hand on Grady, too, as we watched his childlike faith in Christ exude profound joy. It was special to experience.

I wanted my children to know how to truly worship. When I came to Sanyati as a young missionary, I knew little about worship. God taught me in Africa. One particular experience was one I hardly can believe was possible.

The WMU of Gokwe Baptist Church was concerned about one of the members whose husband squandered the family funds on beer. Mrs. Chifanah was a member of the WMU and prayed for her husband faithfully. The group of WMU women had decided that they would come early to visit and encourage this dear woman before a special church service to be held outside her home. Since I would provide the transportation, I loaded up the truck, and the women and I drove to the village.

We parked the truck upon our arrival, and a man at the roadside directed us to walk across a field. When we got to her home, I was surprised to find a dozen or so men there as well.

They were all waiting. Mr. Israel, their former lay leader, was there too, his face wreathed in a big smile. He had ridden 22 miles on his bicycle to the church service. Just a few months earlier, the government had moved all the people in his village to make room for an irrigation system.

Many more people had arrived by the time the service started. We sat down on old sacks and mats under the tree near the Chifanah home and began to sing. A few raindrops fell, and then the rain increased. We had to gather up the mats and move into a sort of breezeway separating the two rooms of the little house. I found myself jammed up in the corner with about 13 women holding babies—the smell of bodies and wet dirt permeating the air. My skirt was not covering my legs properly in the tight space, so one of the women unwrapped the towel around her baby and put it over my legs. Although this was a thoughtful gesture, the towel was damp in spots. I could only imagine what the wetness was from!

Everyone was singing joyously, including me. It was comforting to be with my friends. Then Mr. Israel started to tell the story of the two men traveling on the road to Emmaus. They were talking about Jesus when suddenly He joined them. I was caught up in the story and the meaning. My soul began to rejoice in the presence of the Lord, and my heart worshipped Him. No longer was I thinking about the damp towel or cramped space or the cold wind and rain. Those things no longer mattered. Worship took over. Together, the group worshipped the King of kings and the Lord of lords, and I felt that I was given a glimpse of heaven that morning.

At the end of the service, four young men made public declarations that they wanted to follow Christ. We kept singing and praying, wanting the movement of the Spirit to continue. The time was true fellowship with the Lord.

Before going back to Sanyati, the women gathered around Mrs. Chifanah and gave her a few small gifts. She brought out two clay pots of *mahewu*, a drink made from cornmeal, flour, sugar, millet, and lots of water. Although nonalcoholic, it was a sour drink because it sat for about a day before it was served. In the past, I had been able to graciously decline this beverage and take something else, but in this humble home there was nothing else. Somehow I managed to drink what I was given, smile, and go on my way rejoicing.

That night when Giles and I turned in, I lay in our bed still feeling deeply the presence of the Lord. I had truly worshipped Him with my friends. God was up to something and looking back over it, I think He was preparing the Christians in Rhodesia for the dark and menacing storm rolling in with aggressive ferocity.

Murder at Sanyati

I TRIED TO put the troubling news into the recesses of my mind, but the fact was undeniable—more Catholic missionaries had been brutally killed. We didn't start putting all these murders together as some kind of evil plan until this incident. The attack happened on the side of the road when a car was stopped by guerillas. In the car were a Catholic bishop, a priest, and two nuns on their way to visit a sick friend. The armed terrorists demanded money, and then made them get out of the car after the bishop said that they had none. Once they were out, a man gunned them down after saying, "Missionaries are enemies of the people." At least that was the information reported in the news. One of the nuns survived to testify since she hid by crawling under the car after being shot in the leg.

Just a month before, a Catholic priest from Switzerland was murdered at the Bondolfi Mission in Fort Victoria. We didn't know which nationalist group was responsible for all the deaths, either Robert Mugabe's Zimbabwe African National Union (ZANU) or Joshua Nkomo's Zimbabwe African Peoples Union (ZAPU). Our policy was to stay out of politics and focus on serving Jesus. Both of these groups wanted to overthrow the white government, but they chose violent measures to get attention and accomplish their goals. Many of those fighters, however, were not only intent on killing people of European descent, but they also were determined to kill Christians. It was common for us to hear about attacks on national Christians and pastors far more than on any missionaries. The whole scenario was unsettling.

Then in February 1977, seven Catholic missionaries were murdered, including four nuns. One of the men killed, Brother John, had been a missionary in Rhodesia for 23 years. Other Catholics were slaughtered after this incident. A Dutch Reformed pastor and his wife were victims, making orphans of their six children.

We made a contingency plan with our hospital staff in case Southern Baptist missionaries had to leave at a moment's notice. But evacuation was still something I didn't think would happen. In January 1978, we felt that we had an umbrella of God's protection over the work in Sanyati and Gokwe, although more than a dozen missionaries had been killed over the past year or so. We planned to go on our scheduled furlough in early May of 1978. Everything seemed perfect at the Sanyati Baptist Hospital and our clinics in Gokwe. The outlook for personnel at Sanyati looked bright with two summer missionary workers coming in June; a new doctor to arrive in August; and three journeyman nurses, a lab tech, assistant station manager, and a teacher appointed to educate missionary kids. We already had four doctors, a dentist, three nurses, a pharmacist, and two lab techs who were missionaries, and of course, there were many faithful nationals on our medical staff. Things couldn't have been better as far as staffing. But we were unaware of the storm brewing in the distance.

With four of our sons in the States, we looked forward to our furlough. We were so confident in coming back that we didn't pack up our house and maintained our busy schedule, attending to surgeries and other patients before we left. I put up bread and butter pickles in the pantry for when we planned to come back in 1979. Giles planned to take more anesthesia training in the States. With Grady home from school, since he was going back to the States with us, I packed his suitcase and mine. Late on our last day before furlough, Giles left his work clothes, shoes, and socks in the closet so that he could get to them as soon as we arrived back home in Sanyati. He knew he would be in a hurry to work at the hospital. There were many dreams for our next term on the field. My father had died in 1975, which was still hard for me to deal with, so we would not be going to Louisiana to live. We were headed to Texas.

A Rhodesian friend of the mission and a chaplain in the Rhodesian Armed Services, Norman Woods, came out to Sanyati to make some security suggestions for the station, shortly after we left for furlough on May 9. However, his recommendations had no time to be discussed, and we barely got to the States before a season filled with violence toward missionaries, later known as Bloody June, hit Rhodesia with an intensity that shocked the world.

At least 16 missionaries, mostly Catholic, had been killed over a period of a year and a half; but in June 1978, 20 missionaries or family members were murdered. The first incident that month was on June 2 when 2 Catholic missionaries were killed at a mission station that had a school, close to the Botswana border. Then on June 7, terrorists raided the Salvation Army Usher Institute and killed 2 British female teachers. On the same day, 2 more missionaries were killed in the town of Figtree.

The bloodiest massacre was on June 23, known as the Elim massacre. Eight British Elim Pentecostal missionaries and their young children, including a newborn baby, were abused, beaten, and slaughtered on the Emmanuel Mission School soccer field in the middle of the night. The four young children had been dragged from their beds shortly after 8:30 P.M. The children and adults were savagely beaten with axes, bayonets, and logs. Photos were shown around the world of the atrocities. Who could run a bayonet through the head of a three-week-old baby girl? It made me sick to my stomach to hear the news.

Two more Catholic missionaries were killed on June 29. While these deaths were all tragic and unbelievably horrific, the date in that month that completely changed everything for our mission was June 15, a few days before the Elim massacre.

Archie and Margaret Dunaway lived right across from us on the mission station. They loved to barbeque outside and had created a lovely picnic area on a hill that they leveled behind their house. I was very concerned about Margaret, one of our nurses and the midwife trainer, because not long before we left for furlough, she was diagnosed with breast cancer. Archie was a church developer but also the station manager, whose responsibilities included maintenance and overall upkeep of the station. He kept long hours at the hospital as well. According to one of our missionaries, Archie had received a threatening letter from a terrorist group the week before. I'm not sure exactly what happened the night of June 15, but we learned from several other colleagues of what transpired.

Dr. Maurice and Shirley Randall, two of their children, the Dunaways, John and Mary Monroe, Journeyman Gary Gaunt, three summer interns, and Judy Holtz (the wife of Steve, the MAF pilot who was out of town) were at Sanyati the night of June 15. Nurse Mary Louise Clark was out of town for a meeting, staying with John and Anne Faulkner, missionaries in Que Que. Apparently, Margaret had been working late at the hospital in order to deliver the baby of one of her midwifery students. Because it was after dark, Archie drove the short distance to the hospital with their little dog in the car so that Margaret would not have to walk down the path to their house in the dark and cold, as this occurred during the winter.

The details were sketchy, but Archie got out of the car to investigate a light on in a building that shouldn't have been occupied. Whatever happened, he encountered terrorists who had come onto the property. We had heard that terrorists made it a practice to target a person in charge of a facility. Archie happened to be that person.

About 6:30 P.M., Margaret knocked on the Randalls' door looking for her husband. She had found their car outside the hospital with their dog in it but no Archie. She asked Shirley if Archie had come by. When Shirley said that they had not seen him, she informed her husband, who immediately went out to investigate with Dr. Monroe. What they found was alarming. After not finding Archie at the hospital, they went to the station house where the pumps and maintenance equipment were kept. Archie was not there either, but the fence behind the station house had a hole in it where the wires had been cut.

In the meantime, Margaret told Shirley that she believed her husband was dead. She had seen a vision of his face when she went in their house to look for him. The police department and mission personnel across Rhodesia were contacted, and Margaret insisted that she call her four grown children in the States to tell them that their father was missing, probably dead. Then Margaret started packing because she was convinced that she would be returning to the States.

Shirley, bringing her two sleepy daughters with her, and the other women on the station began a prayer vigil at the Dunaway house. Margaret's house also became the control center with people coming and going all night. Some were helping Margaret pack. Many phone calls had to be made, and the telephone operator kept the Dunaways' party line open, connecting calls when needed. Farmers in the area heard the news by word of mouth and came the next morning, Friday, to help in the search for Archie. The police came at dawn. At 7:15 A.M., Archie's body was found. He had been bayoneted to death, and his battered body had been put under the above-ground root of a tree on the hospital compound.

John Faulkner and Mary Louise Clark arrived at the mission station early that morning. At great risk to their own lives, Pastor and Mrs. Muchechetere had come at daybreak to comfort and stand with the missionaries. Margaret wanted to see her husband's body, although the police discouraged it. Regardless, she did see him. That's when she opened Archie's shirt and saw that he had his long johns on underneath to protect him from the cold. There were four stab wounds, and he had bled internally until he died. He also had been beaten, and his nose was broken. Margaret said quietly, "They treated him just like Jesus. He was stabbed and beaten too."

Steve, the pilot, returned early Friday morning to evacuate his wife, as was MAF policy. Then he returned by plane to evacuate two of the Randall's children, Sheila and Susie. The Randalls put their ten- and eight-year-old daughters on the plane to fly to Gwelo to join their brother and sister, Mark and Sharon, at the missionary kid school hostel. The flight was named the Teddy Bear Special because they quickly boarded the girls at the Sanyati air strip with all their dolls and stuffed animals.

The police wanted to put Archie's body in an open police vehicle, but our missionary men and Margaret finally persuaded the policemen to allow them to load the body in the ambulance in order to take Archie's body to Gatooma.

Also that Friday, the missionaries remaining at Sanyati had to make some quick decisions. The hospital staff was not talking. Apparently they had been scared out of their wits and threatened by the terrorists. Margaret continued packing. The men met together to discuss Margaret's request for a memorial service at Sanyati. She knew how important and respectful it would be in the Shona culture. With Pastor Muchechetere's wise encouragement, the missionaries decided that they would have a memorial the next day before evacuating. It was believed that if they didn't leave, the terrorists would return to destroy the hospital. Persecution had come to Sanyati in full force.

On Saturday, June 17, at the Sanyati Baptist Church, Pastor Muchechetere preached in English, and Bud Fray (who had flown in from South Africa) preached in Shona during the memorial service. Remarkably, Margaret had the strength to say a few words of love and forgiveness. The night before, threats had been made to anyone who attended the funeral, but the church was packed anyway. Everything happened so fast that everyone was still in shock. After the service, all the missionaries in Sanyati left with as many of their possessions they could get in their cars and drove in a caravan to Gwelo. They left the bravest of the staff in charge of the hospital, promising that Dr. Randall and Dr. Monroe would be back for necessary surgeries.

On Sunday afternoon, June 18, in Gwelo, Ralph Bowlin preached at another memorial service held so that mission personnel across Rhodesia could attend. Margaret did not attend this second service since she and one of the summer missionary nurses, Trudy Nash, had flown to Salisbury on Saturday after the first service at the Sanyati Baptist Church. Margaret and Trudy were preparing to fly together from Salisbury to the States.

The week following the funeral, John Faulkner and Jerry Schleiff helped a moving company pack up the rest of the belongings of the Sanyati missionaries into seven trucks. When everything was packed, it was close to dusk. Because they would not be able to get to Gatooma before dark, the Sanyati district commissioner was contacted to ask if the moving company could park the trucks in the commissioner's compound, which had armed security. Permission was granted. The belongings were later taken to storerooms in Salisbury and Gwelo.

Giles and I were just devastated when we were contacted with the news that Archie had been killed and that the missionaries had evacuated Sanyati. Our hearts were heavy with intense grief over Archie's death, Margaret's loss, and the future of the hospital and staff. In fact, our entire mission in Rhodesia was in jeopardy. Then a few days later when we heard about the Elim massacre, we couldn't help but think that the same could have happened at our hospital. Perhaps

Archie prevented the rest of our missionaries and children from being killed. We will never know. With heavy hearts, our colleagues had a called meeting on July 5 to determine what to do—whether to stay or leave the country. Some chose to stay in Rhodesia, some went on furlough, while others chose to leave the country.

Everything had been turned completely upside down. We did not know the future, but we knew that God held the future. Hebrews 13:5–6 became the verses from the Amplified Bible that comforted us: "Be satisfied with your present [circumstances and with what you have]; for He [God] Himself has said, I will not in any way fail you *nor* give you up *nor* leave you without support. [I will] not, [I will] not, [I will] not in any degree leave you helpless *nor* forsake *nor* let [you] down (relax My hold on you)! [Assuredly not!]" No matter what happened, God had a tight grip on us, our colleagues, hospital staff, and our national brothers and sisters across Rhodesia. God was our Helper. He was with Archie and all the other martyrs at the time of their deaths. I had to remind myself more than a few times not to be seized with fear or dread. I worshipped a God who could be trusted. We stayed on our knees in prayer over the dire situation.

We heard about terrible things happening to national believers. Terrorists tried to intimidate villagers by beating family members or friends in front of them. They burned villages, and we even heard of cannibalistic things being done. Ministers were threatened if they continued to preach about Jesus instead of the old tribal gods. Some of our friends had to worship secretly in their huts. Many buried their Bibles to keep guerrillas from destroying them. Some were even murdered, including Archie's assistant, Mr. Cain. Because he stayed on at the mission to run things after Archie's death, one day he did not arrive home after work. His wife and six children began looking for him until they finally heard that terrorists had stopped Mr. Cain on the road while he was on his bicycle, cut off his arms, and threw him into the crocodile-infested river. Another friend of John and Flo Griggs, a young lay preacher, was forced out of his hut in the middle of the night. His young wife hid inside. Outside the hut, guerrillas ranted that he was a sellout because he preached about Jesus, "the white man's God." The young preacher asked them if he could pray but as he knelt, they killed him with a pickax. Many were killed, following the example of the early disciples of Jesus who learned what it meant to be faithful unto death.

Sanyati Baptist Hospital had its 25th anniversary on Christmas Day 1978, probably the most difficult year in its history. The whole country was in a time of transition.

In 1979, the name of the country became Zimbabwe/ Rhodesia, and a black African majority rule came into effect. Later, Rhodesia would be dropped entirely. In August of 1979, the freedom fighters came again to Sanyati and this time ordered staff to close the Sanyati Secondary School. But they did allow the hospital to remain open since the missionaries were not living there. Students were scattered miles away to other town schools and when the primary school was also closed, those young students did not attend school. Pastor

Muchechetere and Chaplain Semwayo were warned that their lives were in danger if they remained at the mission station. They fled, living with relatives in towns. Eventually, Robert Mugabe became the prime minister in 1980, committing to a socialist state, and in 2013 and after 33 years, he is still the leader. Equality for Africans was something that needed to happen, but it was tragic that violence was the way the government and laws changed. Rev. Semwayo and Rev. Muchechetere both moved back to Sanyati with their families in 1980. Bud and Jane's son, Jeff, a recent college graduate, was the first from our mission to move back to help for a few months.

Being in the States while all this happened brought mixed emotions. We wanted to be with our colleagues and national friends at this time of need, but we also didn't have the traumatic experiences to deal with in the same way as our friends. We kept getting reports from the Randalls that Maurice and John were flying into or driving to Sanyati once or twice a week for surgeries, but none of our missionaries had returned to live permanently in Sanyati.

Life had continued, however. Our son, David, married Laurel and continued his path toward being a doctor, passing his boards and doing surgical residency at Baylor. Our son, Giles, and his wife were expecting a baby, and eventually Amy came to live with us temporarily in Texas before the baby was born while Giles stayed working as a doctor in Colorado. Gordon finished up at Texas A&M University and attended Southwestern Baptist Theological Seminary while continuing to pastor the Macedonia-Hix Baptist Church near College Station, Texas. Gregg was at Texas A&M University and had been ordained as a minister. He met Donna, and they married in 1980. Gregg pastored Harmony Baptist Church near Caldwell, Texas, while finishing his degree at A&M. Grady attended a state school in Texas while we were on furlough since my husband was in a term of study in anesthesiology. We desperately wanted to go back to Sanyati, but because of the new government, we were delayed in leaving the States because it had become difficult to get work permits.

I can't tell you how many people in the States told us we should not go back to Africa. But how can someone else determine God's will for our lives? We knew God wanted us to return to finish our missionary career. Because of the unrest in the country where we served, we assumed that was why we were asked to address the Southern Baptist Convention for the FMB in June 1980. Gordon and David also spoke with us. The persecution of Christians became an issue of prayer, and we knew that God was hearing the prayers of His people. Two months after the Convention, August 1980, we returned to Zimbabwe but not to Sanyati. It was the most disappointing change of our lives. Giles ended up teaching anesthesiology at the medical college in Harare (the new name for Salisbury), Grady went back to his boarding school in Bulawayo, and my professional career as a doctor, for the most part, ended. It was not an easy pill to swallow, especially since I was asked to take over the business and treasury duties of the mission. That task was not my idea of fun, but I needed something to do.

Chapter 13

Our belongings in Sanyati had been packed up for us very quickly after Archie's death while we were in the States. We settled into one of the houses our mission owned in Harare, trying to catch news here and there concerning people in the Sanyati Reserve. How I longed to go to Sanyati! One of our friends, Pastor Musiyiwa, who had been the former assistant to Chaplain Semwayo at Sanyati Baptist Hospital and then the chaplain of the Gokwe clinics, had to flee with his family from their home with only the clothes on their backs during the high point of the war at the end of the 1970s. He became the pastor of a church in 1980 and helped to plan a big evangelistic crusade for the country. Gregg was invited by him to preach in the crusade. Thus, in September of 1981, Gregg and Donna came to Zimbabwe. More than 2,000 decisions were made for Christ, and as I listened to my son preach in fluent Shona, I began to sense that God would use my children to continue the task of telling others in Africa about our precious Jesus.

While Gregg was still in the country, he, Donna, and I traveled to Sanyati. I had not been back since May 1978. When we drove on The Road and off the beaten path, we saw the devastation and mark of the terrorists. Churches, shops, villages, schools, and community buildings were destroyed. Gregg was asked to preach at our Baptist church in Kasirisiri, but there was no building. We met under the trees beside the bits and pieces of the building's foundation. One woman told me that her husband had been killed just like Archie, and she had been left with nine children. Other men from the church had been tortured and murdered. Since the school close by also was demolished, the children and teachers met under trees. In the midst of this devastation, God confirmed to Gregg and Donna that they were to come back to Gregg's homeland to be missionaries. I always believed that Gregg was our "son of the people," and it seemed only right that he would want to return.

The reunion with friends at the Sanyati Baptist Hospital was very emotional. The Randalls had returned in December 1980, and several other missionaries had moved back since then as well. The hospital had been turned over to the Baptist Convention of Zimbabwe under a hospital board of directors, later receiving financial help from the government. Some medical missionary personnel were permitted to serve. During the time after the murder, the hospital never closed. The national staff were the ones who bravely kept things going after Archie's death. I walked through the hospital and my heart melted. The staff showed us where Archie's body was found as we reheard the story. It was difficult not to break down in sobs. We also talked about Margaret, who had passed away just a few months before because of the cancer.

There is no other explanation to how we got through those years after that timely furlough in 1978 except God. Over the years, God got us through the tragic deaths of two of Clyde Dotson's wives, Archie's death, our inability to return to Sanyati, the death of Clyde Dotson himself, and the untimely death of young Chip Corley, son of colleagues Charles and Gayla. Time and time again, God spoke to me from His Word, especially from Ephesians 3, that He "is able to do exceedingly abundantly above all that we ask or think, according to the power that works in us."

By the time 1983 came, we had been tested and tried. God had taught us complete and utter dependence upon Him. Psalm 84:5–6 took on a life of its own when I realized that because my strength was in Him, He would make my valley of weeping into a place of springs. His presence would get us over the next hurdle.

CHAPTER 14

A Time to Love

"OLD AGE DOES not announce itself," goes the Zulu proverb, and after 30 years as missionaries in Africa, Giles and I were beginning to feel our age when we came to the States on furlough in 1983. Gordon was to be married to Leigh Ann Harrison, a former journeyman to South Africa, and we had grandchildren, Daniel and Katie, to see. Three of our children were in the process of seeking God about missionary service in Africa. Our hearts were filled with joy!

We were not ready to retire and hoped to return to Africa and stay long enough to see our children serve in Africa while we were there. Therefore, going back to Harare after furlough was easier this time, accepting that the most doctoring I would do would be once a week at a little clinic not far from where we lived. Giles continued in his teaching position at the medical college and his status at hospitals in Harare. We felt privileged to still be able to serve our Lord in Zimbabwe.

But Giles became unable to function as a doctor due to what we thought were minor health issues, so he focused on finishing out our term as an administrator for the mission. I noticed that Giles had difficulty walking, and he experienced pain in his neck and back. We discovered that some of the disks in his neck were greatly diminished, and a cervical traction apparatus was sent to Giles from the States for his use. I watched my dear husband basically live in pain. Muscle spasms in his legs kept him from sleeping, and there was no way to relieve the spasms in his neck, upper back, and shoulders. Then his neck became contorted.

With no more options for the necessary medical attention in Zimbabwe, I flew to Dallas, Texas, with Giles in 1986 so that he could have neck surgery. That was when he was diagnosed with axial dystonia, a condition causing involuntary muscle contractions resulting in twisted posture. This diagnosis prevented Giles's immediate return to Africa. We were saddened to receive this news, but more than anything I wanted Giles to be out of the intense pain. Giles wasn't my only concern, however. Having no idea that we would not return as scheduled to Zimbabwe, we left Grady to continue his education and group setting in the Sir Humphrey Gibbs Training Centre in Bulawayo. And here we were halfway across the world from him! Our plan had been to return to Zimbabwe within four to six weeks after our arrival in the States. We basically just locked the house in Harare and left, just as we did when we left Sanyati in 1978 for our furlough.

I claimed the verses in Philippians 4:6–7: "Be anxious for nothing, but in everything by prayer and supplication, with thanksgiving, let your requests be made known to God; and the peace of God, which surpasses all understanding, will guard your hearts and minds through Christ Jesus." I quoted those verses at night in order to relax enough to sleep. Eventually we worked it out for missionary friends to board and care for Grady during school holidays so that he could stay at his school until I could get back to Zimbabwe. I returned to Africa in August 1986 to get Grady and pack up the few belongings we wanted to keep. God's grace was sufficient, as well as the help we received from our mission.

After 33 years of missionary service on the field, our time in Africa was coming to a close. Of course, we got Grady to the States, and Giles and I began the journey of my husband's debilitating condition. In God's mercy and grace, it was time to pass the baton to our sons. He gave us the privilege of seeing three of our boys and their wives minister in Africa as missionaries—David as a doctor and later psychiatrist in Ghana, Gordon as a church planter and administrator in Botswana and Zimbabwe, and Gregg as a church planter in Zimbabwe. God blessed us with five wonderful sons, four daughters-in-law, eventually 14 grandchildren, and even great grandchildren—several of whom are doctors or ministers.

Miraculously, toward the close of 1987, Giles and I were able to return to Zimbabwe together for a few months to say our final good-byes and before our official retirement in September of 1988. We attended a prayer retreat with our colleagues and visited our dear national friends. While at a special service held in our honor at one of the Baptist churches, a teacher friend from Sanyati was speaking and asked the audience a rhetorical question, What is the greatest gift our doctors have given us? My mind raced with answers that perhaps would be remembered such as our medical expertise, the long hours of hospital work, our service in national churches, or our partnership with the Baptist Convention of Zimbabwe and WMU. But none of those things was the answer the teacher gave. Instead, he continued, "It was their open home that was open to everyone, even in the years of Prime Minister Ian Smith when it was not acceptable (for a white family to open their home to a black man or woman). Their children and ours were friends together in our homes or their home. Now their son Gregg is our missionary and truly one of us. Yes, their home and their sons are our doctors' greatest gift to us."

Giles and I were humbled, because the plain truth of the matter is that I am naturally a doer of tasks, not one who just loves on people. At least I didn't think so. Whatever love was shown, God did this through us. He was faithful. He was the lover. His ways superseded my natural tendencies. To demonstrate love, of course one opens his or her home! How could we have done anything less?

There is certainly nothing special about me. I don't have the corner of the market on anything. Only God could take a little, country girl from Catahoula Hills like me and accomplish His will and show His love. Any honor and glory unquestionably belong to Him. Obviously, He can take a weak vessel of clay, even a cracked pot, and let His light shine through her to demonstrate that God loves the world. He does. He loves the world far more than I ever could. He wants the people groups of the world to come to know Him personally. He wants people to accept His love and forgiveness, even when they don't believe God could ever love or forgive them. God is in the business of changing lives. He transformed mine. He draws people to Himself, and He sends them to tell the story of Jesus. How can we not love other people and tell them about Jesus after what He has done for us? All those years ago when God spoke to me on the porch of my house, behind the piano at church, and at Ridgecrest in the Sunday School room and prayer garden, did He know how my life would turn out? Yes, He did. My life is full because whatever love has been shown through my life is due to the fact that He loves me. His love for His followers is an awesome thought to ponder.

It has been more than 25 years since our retirement from missionary service. If I had to choose all over again, I would choose the same path. No question. There's an African proverb that says, "If old age stops the hunter from going hunting, he must be content with telling his ancient exploits." Maybe that's what I've done on these pages. Without a doubt, God's love, not my story, is what lasts.

Group Discussion Questions

CHAPTER 1

1. What were positive parenting qualities of Wana Ann's parents that helped form her as a child?

2. Even though Wana Ann's family struggled financially, what did Wana Ann focus her attention on as a girl?

3. What was the process of Wana Ann's conversion? How did she know that one day God would use her to help others?

4. What can you learn that might help you as a parent? As a seeker of God's will?

CHAPTER 2

1. Describe how Wana Ann began to rely more on prayer in her spiritual walk and how that affected learning of God's will for her career.

2. How did God work in Wana Ann's future concerning a mate?

3. How did God deal with Wana Ann about pride, and how did she respond to God? How did God reward her later concerning medical school?

4. What obstacles did Wana Ann have to overcome to see God's plan accomplished in getting her medical degree? What can you learn from this?

CHAPTER 3

1. What were Wana Ann's initial impressions of the Sanyati Reserve from what she heard about it? What was the reality of Sanyati? When and how did she begin to understand that God was calling her to Sanyati?

2. What did you learn from Wana Ann's experience with her father's initial lack of support of her missions endeavors? If you are a parent, what might you have done differently? If you are a future missionary, what might you do if you were to have this response from a parent?

3. How did Scripture speak to Giles and Wana Ann concerning financial gain as doctors in the States?

4. What were Wana Ann's concerns about going to Sanyati once she did more research on the country of Southern Rhodesia?

5. How could fear have immobilized Wana Ann, if she had allowed it? How does fear affect you in following God's will?

CHAPTER 4

1. How hard do you think it was for Wana Ann to say good-bye to family and why? How do you think you would feel?

2. When crossing into Rhodesia, how did Wana Ann feel? When you are faced with a new change in life, what can you learn from Wana Ann's response to change?

3. How did Wana Ann deal with prejudice and the treatment of others? What prejudice do you have in your life?

CHAPTER 5

1. Describe how Wana Ann faced the primitive conditions of Sanyati.

2. What did God teach Wana Ann through the experience with her first patient?

3. What was the name Wana Ann received, and what was her response?

4. How did God encourage Wana Ann after she delivered a stillborn baby but saved the life of the mother?

5. What was Wana Ann reminded of over and over that kept her from giving up her missionary call?

CHAPTER 6

1. How did the Forts face the prevalent witchcraft in the area?

2. How can cultural beliefs sometimes be a barrier to the hearing of the gospel? How did the Forts compensate for this problem?

3. What truth did Wana Ann learn from Psalm 23?

4. What did Wana Ann learn about spiritual warfare? How can you apply these truths?

CHAPTER 7

1. How important was it that Wana Ann and Giles developed strong friendships with Africans?

2. Areas distant from Sanyati became of interest to the Forts and other missionaries and national pastors. What steps did they take in these early years for future work in these remote places?

3. What spiritual warfare and tragedies did the Forts and the mission face in their first term of service?

4. How have you felt after experiencing tragedy? How have you coped?

CHAPTER 8

1. What good things were happening at Sanyati
   Baptist Hospital?

2. What was it like for Wana Ann to return to the States
   for furlough? How was it evident that Sanyati had also
   become their home?

3. What was Wana Ann's view of Job 1:21? How can the
   truth of this verse be applied to your life?

CHAPTER 9

1. What did you learn about forgiveness and mercy from
   the story of Jeri Muvindi?

2. How did John 10 reinforce Wana Ann's missionary call?

3. How did friends encourage Wana Ann in her own
   spiritual walk?

4. Should circumstances control your outlook on life? If
   not, what should?

CHAPTER 10

1. What did God teach Wana Ann when she was
   introduced to Grady?

2. How did 1 Thessalonians 5:18 and the spiritual lessons
   God was teaching Wana Ann through Grady help her

cope with the news of the plane crash? How can you apply this truth in your life?

3. What are a few parenting skills that were helpful to the Forts?

4. What sacrifices did Wana Ann have to make?

CHAPTER 11

1. What can you learn about God through the healing of Lillian?

2. Why is it important to pray for missionaries and their work?

3. State specific requests found in David's prayer in Psalm 24:4–15.

CHAPTER 12

1. How did Wana Ann face the enemy head on when confronting the demon-possessed woman?

2. How did Wana Ann best lead others to Christ?

3. Explain the revelation Sophie had about God's love.

4. Explain one story about Wana Ann learning to worship.

Group Discussion Guide

CHAPTER 13

1. Even though missionaries were being murdered before the Forts' furlough in 1978, did the Forts feel like anything would happen to their station and why?

2. How did Archie's death change everything for the Forts?

3. How did Hebrews 13:5–6 comfort the Forts?

4. How can well-meaning people distract missionaries from God's call on their lives?

CHAPTER 14

1. What Bible verses did Wana Ann quote many times after Giles's debilitating diagnosis?

2. What were Wana Ann and Giles known for by the Africans who honored them at retirement?

3. According to Wana Ann, what lasts in this world?

4. What is the most meaningful truth you learned from this book?

Phonetic Pronunciation Guide*

ambuyas: ahm-BOO-yahz

Ayorinde: ah-your-RIN-day

Bandomu: bahn-DOE-moo

Blace: BLAH-say

Bloemfontein: BLOOM-fon-tain

Busvumani: boo-soo-MAHN-nee

Changamire: chahng-gah-MEE-ray

Chifanah: chee-FAH-nah

Chironga: chee-RONE-gah

ChiSezuru: chee-say-ZOO-roo

Chisikwa: chee-SEE-qua

Gatooma: gah-TOOM-mah

Gokwe: GO-quay

Gutu: GOO-too

Gwelo: GWEY-low

Gweru: GWEY-roo

Harare: hah-RAH-eh

Kadoma: ka-DOME-mah

Kasirisiri: kah-see-ree-SEE-ree

kraal: crawl

Lezu: LAY-zoo

Lobengula: low-ben-GOO-lah

Lozi: LOW-zee

machilla: ma-CHEE-la

mahewu: mah-HAY-woo

Mai Chiremba: my-EE chee-REM-bah

Mairos: mah-EE-rose

Maposa: mah-POE-sah

Maranke: mah-RAHN-kay

Mashona: mah-SHOW-nah

Matabele: mah-tah-BEH-lee

midzimu: mid-ZEE-moo

Moyana: moy-YAH-nah

Mtange: em-TAHN-geh

Muchechetere: moo-cheh-cheh-TARE-ray

Mufundisi: moo-foon-DEE-see

Mugabe: moo-GAH-bay

Munyaradizi: moon-yah-rah-DEE-zee

musha: MOO-shah

Musiyiwa: moo-see-YEE-wah

Mutapa: moo-TAH-pah

muti: MOO-tee

Muvindi: moo-VIN-dee

Mwari: MWAH-ree

Mzilikazi: em-ZEE-lee-KAH-zee

Ndau: en-DOW

Ndebele: en-dah-BELL-lay

Nenyuka: nen-YOU-kah

Neuso: nay-OO-so

Ngoma: en-GO-mah

Ngomo: en-GO-mow

Ngoni: en-GO-nee

Nguni: en-GOO-nee

Nkomo: nen-CO-mow

Nyasaland: nigh-AH-sah-land

Nyathi: NYAHT-ee

Nyekanyeka: NYAY-can-YAY-kah

Nziramasanga: nzeer-ah-mah-SAHN-gah

putzi: POOT-zee

Que Que (Kwekwe): QUAY-quay

Rimuka: ree-MOO-kah

Rozwi: ROSE-wee

Sanyati: sahn-YAH-tee

Semchembu: sim-CHIM-boo

Semwayo: sim-WAY-yo

Shangaan: SHAHN-gahn

Shangwe: SHAHNG-way

Shona: SHOW-nah

Sindebele: Sin-dah-BELL-lay

Sithole: sit-TOE-lay

Sotho: SOO-too

Tonga: TONG-gah

Umtali: oom-TAH-lee

Venandi: vin-NAHN-dee

Whozhele: hoe-ZELL-lay

Wiri: WEE-ree

Zimbabwe: zim-BOB-way

*Gregg and Donna Fort, contributors

WANA ANN'S WONDER FRUIT COBBLER

½ cup flour
½ cup sugar
Pinch of salt
1 teaspoon baking powder
½ cup milk

Mix or sift together flour, sugar, salt, and baking powder. Add milk and mix well. Empty 1 can of fruit into a greased 8-by-8 glass pan. Pour flour and milk mixture over fruit. Dot with 2 tablespoons of butter. Bake about 30 minutes at 350°F.

Photo Descriptions

CHAPTER 1

Firstborn Wana Ann with her six sisters of the Gibson family.

CHAPTER 2

Wana Ann graduated summa cum laude from Louisiana Tech on October 18, 1944. She is pictured with her parents, David Wanamaker and Izetta Gibson.

CHAPTER 3

Giles, a graduate of Texas A&M University, is pictured in his uniform.

CHAPTER 4

Giles and Wana Ann Fort, ready to start their adventurous life.

CHAPTER 5

Giles and Wana Ann pictured in one of their early surgical procedures.

CHAPTER 6

Giles and Wana Ann performing surgery, assisted by an African nurse.

CHAPTER 7

A cluster of huts (*kraal*) in remote Zimbabwe.

CHAPTER 8

Wana Ann, a beautiful woman, inside and out.

CHAPTER 9

Wana Ann loved her friends. Two of her Zimbabwean friends were Mrs. Nyathi (*far left*) and Mrs. Ndlovu (*second from left*). Wana Ann is on the far right.

CHAPTER 10

Fort Family: (*top row*) Giles III (*left to right*), David, and Gordon, (*front row*) Giles Jr., Grady, Wana Ann, and Gregg

CHAPTER 11

A crowd of worshippers gather at the Sanyati Baptist Church.

CHAPTER 12

Patients listen intently to morning devotions broadcast on the hospital's intercom system.

CHAPTER 13

Aerial view of Sanyati Baptist Hospital.

CHAPTER 14

Wana Ann and Giles retire in 1988 after nearly 36 years of missionary service.

About the Authors

Pioneer Southern Baptist missionary to Zimbabwe, DR. *WANA ANN G. FORT*, with her doctor husband, Giles, launched a spiritual awakening through medical missions at the Sanyati Baptist Hospital where they were the first doctors in 1953. Through nearly 36 years of missionary service with the IMB, countless people came to Christ. One of three female graduates of Baylor University College of Medicine in 1949 and recipient of their Distinguished Alumni Award in 1990, Wana Ann is a contributor to books such as *Dream Builder* and *A History of Medical Missions*. She raised five sons in Africa with her late husband and currently resides in Baton Rouge, Louisiana.

Kim P. Davis is a writer who served 13 years in Africa as an IMB missionary with her husband and two of Dr. Fort's sons. She has compiled such books as *Voices of the Faithful* and *Voices of the Faithful, Book Two,* and is the author of *My Life, His Mission.* She is a graduate of the University of Georgia's Henry W. Grady School of Journalism. Kim and her husband, D. Ray, have three grown children and live in Richmond, Virginia.

In the back of this book, you will find a page regarding Worldcrafts, which the writer had a brief involvement with in Zimbabwe. She writes, "In the late 1990s, a small group of women and IMB missionary in Harare, Zimbabwe, began to pray about and discussed how they might raise money to construct a church building for Parktown Baptist Church. Most of the church members lived on meager wages due to the high unemployment rate in the country. WorldCrafts became the answer to their prayers. With the women's craft skills, they started making simple aprons in exotic African print for WorldCrafts, all while sewing joyfully together under the roof of the temporary church building of asbestos and chicken wire. Over the years, the women added more items to the catalog, giving much of the money to the church and using some to feed their families."

WorldCrafts^{SM} develops sustainable, fair-trade businesses among impoverished people around the world. Each WorldCrafts product represents lives changed by the opportunity to earn an income with dignity and to hear the offer of everlasting life.

Visit WorldCrafts.org to learn more about WorldCrafts artisans, hosting WorldCrafts parties and to shop!

WORLDCRAFTS^{SM}
Committed. Holistic. Fair Trade.
WorldCrafts.org 1-800-968-7301

WorldCrafts is a division of WMU®.